SCENES FROM THE CITY
FILMMAKING IN NEW YORK 1966–2006

Published by
Rizzoli International Publications, Inc.
300 Park Avenue South
New York, New York 10010
www.rizzoliusa.com

The opinions expressed here belong to individuals and do not necessarily represent the views of the New York City Mayor's Office of Film, Theatre and Broadcasting.

2006 2007 2008 2009 / 10 9 8 7 6 5 4 3 2

Printed in China

ISBN 10: 0-8478-2890-5
ISBN 13: 978-0847-8289-06

Distributed by Random House

Library of Congress Catalog Control Number: 2006924103

SCENES FROM THE CITY
FILMMAKING IN NEW YORK 1966–2006

**EDITED BY
JAMES SANDERS**

**CONTRIBUTIONS BY
MARTIN SCORSESE
AND NORA EPHRON**

**PRODUCED WITH
THE MAYOR'S OFFICE
OF FILM, THEATRE
AND BROADCASTING**

RIZZOLI
NEW YORK

A location is as important as a character in a movie. The great thing about New York City is that to *know* New York… is impossible, because it is too vast. But you can be certain of one thing…no matter where you look, there's a shot. Anywhere you look, it's interesting.

Peter Bogdanovich, director

Filming ACROSS THE SEA OF TIME (1995)

In New York, you should be able to find a location which not only gives you what you need, but with a little luck gives you more than what you need—gives you an extra dimension that you never thought possible.

Sidney Lumet, director

Filming DOG DAY AFTERNOON (1973)

It's all there to see on the streets of New York.

Tim Robbins, actor and producer

Filming SIX DEGREES OF
SEPARATION (1993)

There was always, from the inception of the Mayor's Film Office–and still very much part of its underlying mission–the idea that having New York on the silver screen, having its presence around the world, creates part of the magic and the myth and the lure of the city. Films help make New York the "city of dreams," the place people want to come to as one of the great destinations in the world–and want to come to because of the fantasy of all those films they saw, films "made in New York."

Jon Kamen, producer

Filming DEATH TO SMOOCHY (2002)

TABLE OF CONTENTS

Forty years ago, in the summer of 1966, my predecessor Mayor John V. Lindsay established the Mayor's Office of Film, Theatre and Broadcasting—the first agency of its kind in the world.

In the decades since, the Mayor's Office has helped spark an extraordinary renaissance in motion picture and television production in New York, giving rise in turn to one of the most successful and significant industries in the city, today employing over one hundred thousand New Yorkers and representing more than five *billion* dollars a year in economic activity.

Film and television production is a glamorous business, associated in the public mind with world-famous stars, directors, and other celebrities. But it is also a genuine industry, whose vast majority of jobs are filled with lesser-known but no less dedicated craftsmen and technicians, including camera operators, electricians, sound engineers, editors, art directors, makeup and wardrobe artists, location scouts, carpenters, grips, drivers, and background talent—to name just a few of the literally hundreds of different occupations needed to produce feature films and television.

The benefits to the city from this activity are enormous. Beyond the hundred thousand New Yorkers the movie and television industry employs directly, it indirectly helps to support many tens of thousands more, by utilizing more than four thousand local businesses across the five boroughs—all of which helps bring in additional revenues to support crucial city services that benefit all New Yorkers.

It is for these reasons that the city is pleased to be a major supporter of our local entertainment industry. For four decades, the Mayor's Office of Film, Theatre and Broadcasting has been an important ally of every production that has shot in New York, including the many feature films and television shows featured in this volume. Throughout this time, the city has continued to offer an array of services and benefits for producers that remains unique: a free "one stop" permit for location shooting, free police assistance, free access to city locations and parks, and free parking. We like to say we assist producers with every phase of production—from script to screen—and have gained a well-earned reputation in the industry for finding ways to say "yes."

I am especially proud of the extraordinary success the city has enjoyed in attracting film and television production over the past four years, thanks in large part to the tireless efforts of our Film Commissioner Katherine Oliver and her hardworking, dedicated staff at the Mayor's Office, the crucial assistance provided every day of the year by the NYPD's Movie and TV Unit, and the immense support we have received from local studios, labor unions, and creative members of the industry all across New York City.

Our work is far from done. Recognizing the increased levels of competition for business in recent years, we have embarked on several

Mayor Bloomberg makes his television debut on the "Made in NY" production "Law & Order," currently the longest running drama series on primetime television, in a scene taped in the Blue Room at City Hall.

Photo: Ed Reed

major initiatives to make New York even larger and more active as a production center. In January 2005, to expand business further, I signed the "Made in NY" tax credit into law, marking the first time the city offered such a production incentive. This includes a 15 percent refundable tax credit from the city and state for qualified feature films and television shows produced in the city. The Mayor's Office also introduced the "Made in NY" marketing program, which leverages the city's existing assets by providing free advertising on city property to productions which shoot here, and the "Made in NY" discount card, which offers active productions discounts at hundreds of vendors throughout the five boroughs—at once lowering the cost of production in the city and driving revenue to local communities.

The results of these programs and initiatives have exceeded expectations. The number of location production days in 2005 jumped 35 percent over the previous year to reach 31,570 days—the largest number on record since the Mayor's Film Office began. Meanwhile, the dramatic expansion of stage space and other facilities now underway at the city's three major studios helps to assure that New York will retain its status as one of the world's greatest centers of film and television production.

In the end, the entertainment industry's greatest contribution to the city is to make the image and idea of New York a living, thrilling presence in the minds of people around the world. Few other cities on earth—if any—have been celebrated more widely or memorably onscreen than New York. In that sense, the industry can be considered a priceless marketing tool for the city, helping to draw millions of visitors and tourists each year to New York—further propelling its economy, prosperity, and vitality.

We look forward to many more years of helping film and television artists and professionals bring the magic of our city to audiences across the globe.

MICHAEL R. BLOOMBERG
Mayor
The City of New York
2006

I was thrilled when Mayor Michael Bloomberg asked me in the summer of 2002 to become commissioner of the Mayor's Office of Film, Theatre and Broadcasting. Having had the privilege of working with the Mayor for many years in the private sector—most recently as General Manager of Bloomberg, LP—I thought I had a good idea of what his approach and expectations would be, and was enormously pleased to be handed one of the most significant—and exciting—responsibilities in city government.

It was a daunting moment. That year, with the city still emerging from the trauma of September 11, New York's production business—while having made enormous strides over the previous decade—was facing serious difficulties. As a media executive himself, the Mayor was well aware of the problems facing the industry—but also knew that film and television production remained an extremely viable business for New York, with plenty of opportunity for growth. His first advice was to build on the strengths of what New York had to offer. He said to me: energize the office, simplify the process, resurrect the industry. He also said, make it fun. Go for the "wow" factor, and make a statement. He knew that although filmmaking is an important economic activity, it is also an exciting and magical way of life, a special world unto itself, with its own heritage and traditions.

It is in that spirit that we conceived of the idea of the illustrated volume you hold in your hand. *Scenes from the City* was created to provide an inside look at one of the most exciting spectacles in the world: the location filmmaking that takes place daily all around the five boroughs of New York City. As assembled and edited by the architect and writer James Sanders, the striking images in *Scenes from the City* together tell the story of New York's continual transfiguration, over the past four decades, into what has been called "the biggest backlot in the world."

And what a story it is! From the impressive early outpouring of films in the late 1960s and 1970s—*Midnight Cowboy*, *The French Connection*, *The Producers*, *Rosemary's Baby*, *Klute*, among many others—to the rise of the great New York-based filmmakers in the 1970s and 80s (including Martin Scorsese, Woody Allen, Spike Lee, and our beloved veteran, Sidney Lumet), to the birth of an influential "independent" film industry in the late 1980s and 1990s as an alternative to mainstream studio production, to the ever larger and more complex use of the city by studio films themselves (including the amazing utilization of real locations for jaw-dropping spectacles and special effects), the history of location filming in New York is nothing short of an epic—and crucial—chapter in the history of American movies themselves.

All along, the Mayor's Office of Film, Theatre and Broadcasting has been there, assisting literally every production that has shot on the streets and public spaces of the city over the past forty years, from big studio films to small independent features, as well as television series and made-for-TV movies, commercials, music videos, children's

Commissioner Katherine Oliver promotes the release of the "Made in NY" production *Spider-Man 2* on "The Today Show" with Tobey Maguire and schoolchildren selected to implement volunteer plans in their communities as part of the "Little Apple Heroes" contest sponsored by Columbia Pictures and the MOFTB.

shows, live programming, and a stunning variety of other kinds of projects—many of which make an appearance in the pages of this book.

To this day, nothing gives me greater pleasure than the chance to sit down and work closely with some of the greatest producers and directors in the business to help make their cinematic visions possible—including some of the most unusual and unlikely ones. Over the years, the Mayor's Office has consistently arranged for locations that no one would have thought possible—closing the Brooklyn Bridge for the production of *Stay*, shutting Times Square for *Vanilla Sky*, or lobbying to help *The Interpreter* become the first film in more than half a century to shoot inside the United Nations. Once the coordination and paperwork is done and the shooting starts, I love stopping by the set, to see the army of dedicated crew members—often assisted closely by the hard working and experienced members of our own New York Police Department's Movie and TV Unit—turning the streets and open spaces of the city into the setting for another filmic moment, destined to make its appearance, many months hence, on movie or television screens all around the world.

It is this same sense of excitement and wonder that we have sought to convey and communicate in the pages of this book, which attempts to bring to life once again many of the unforgettable scenes and films that have emerged from the streets and sidewalks of New York over the past forty years. At the same time, we hope the book will serve to educate and enlighten the public about the remarkable heritage of film production in the city, offering a glimpse of the filmmaking process and of the insights of the filmmakers themselves. Taken together, the text and images are intended to underscore not only the ongoing activities of the Mayor's Office and the extraordinary inventory of locations to be found around the five boroughs, but the astonishing commitment, talent, and dedication that generations of moviemakers have demonstrated as they transformed the city of New York into one of the world's most compelling cinematic settings.

KATHERINE OLIVER
Commissioner
The City of New York
Mayor's Office of Film, Theatre and Broadcasting
2006

ON LOCATION IN NEW YORK 1966–2006
BY JAMES SANDERS

Out on the Streets

If you are a Los Angeles filmmaker you are going to shoot on stage, but New York has always been about being out there on the streets. From *On the Waterfront* to Scorsese, John Cassavetes, Sidney Lumet, Woody Allen. Because what is a better set than New York City?
SPIKE LEE, DIRECTOR, 2005

On May 31, 1966, in City Hall, New York's Mayor John V. Lindsay issued a memorandum known as Executive Order Number 10. Just three typescript pages long, the document laid out an impressive array of new initiatives to encourage film and television production in New York, including the outlines of a new city office—the first of its kind in the world—to assist producers working in the five boroughs. In a real sense, the document marked the birth of the agency known today as the Mayor's Office of Film, Theatre and Broadcasting. But it also marked a crucial step in what was perhaps the greatest and most fundamental transformation, across the entire twentieth century, in the way movies are made.

Since the time of World War I, feature film production in most countries had been centered on the great indoor-outdoor production facilities known as studios. In the United States, ironically, the rise of the studio system had caused Los Angeles to supersede New York City as the nation's center of film production. It had been New York where American movies had come into being around the start of the twentieth century, when a handful of fledgling companies (Edison, Biograph, and Vitagraph) began shooting documentary-style "actuality" films on the streets of Manhattan, then opened the nation's first movie studios in the distant reaches of the Bronx, Brooklyn, and (a few years later) Queens. But by the end of the 1920s, the production of feature films in America had relocated almost completely to the sprawling complexes of stages, sheds, and outdoor sets—each a hundred acres or more in size—springing up across the suburbs of Los Angeles. From here would emerge the great studio-created features that dominated American film production—and capture the imagination of the world—for the next fifty years or more.

To be sure, New York did not disappear from the screen during those years. Far from it. Within the confines of the studios, a glittering, stylized "mythic city" arose in the early 1930s, constructed on sound stages and backlots, and brought to life in some of the most memorable films of the century, from *42nd Street* and *King Kong* to *Swing Time* and *Dead End*. But in the last months of World War II and the first years afterward, a handful of Hollywood producers and directors began exploring a daring alternative: taking their cameras onto the streets of the city itself, to create films—or at least sequences—not only set but *shot* in New York.

They were not alone, of course. In Italy during those same years, a group of gifted filmmakers—Roberto Rossellini, Vittorio de Sica, Luchino Visconti—were pioneering a similarly innovative approach called neorealism—in part because the war-torn conditions of the time gave them no choice. Their efforts, in turn, would be taken up a decade later by the influential directors of France's "New Wave": Jean-Luc Godard, François Truffaut, Claude Chabrol, Jacques Rivette, and Eric Rohmer. Like the Italians before them, the French filmmakers took their crews and equipment out of the studio and into the sidewalks, parks, cafés, shops, and bedrooms of the city. Using a new generation of lightweight Eclair cameras, they replaced carefully composed sound-stage setups with long, mobile (even handheld), semi-improvised takes in actual locations, and, wherever possible, jettisoned highly stylized stage lighting for the relatively flat and even illumination of what Godard's cinematographer Raoul Coutard called "the light of day."

Thus by the mid-1960s, some of the most talented and forward-looking filmmakers on both continents had begun making a historic shift away from the confines of the studio—and the traditional conventions of studio production—and toward a new approach, one that would seek to turn the entire city into a kind of outdoor stage. As late as 1965, however, that seismic transformation remained constrained, in America at least, by the nightmarish difficulties—logistical and administrative—of shooting on location. It was in that context that Mayor Lindsay's three-page interagency memo, intended primarily to encourage greater employment and activity in the city's production business, would help to ignite a revolution in American filmmaking—one that would soon transform the relationship of New York and the film industry, the relationship of cities and film as a whole, and, within a remarkably short space of time, the nature of American movies themselves.

Nothing But Talk

In spite of all the talk, I don't think you will find an average of more than two or three top pictures a year turned out here. New York City has had a great opportunity in recent years to become the center of the entire motion picture industry, but our city administration has done nothing to encourage it, and has done a great deal to hinder it. The situation is nothing short of stupid.

[In Los Angeles], motion picture companies get immediate cooperation from the city government. Here they get nothing but talk.

MAX YOUNGSTEIN, FILM PRODUCER, 1964

From today's perspective, the notion of a film commission seems an obvious, self-evident one. Certainly it is common enough. South Dakota has a film commission, as does South Carolina, Saskatchewan, Singapore, Switzerland, and South Korea. There are, in fact, over 300 municipal, territorial, and national film commissions in more than thirty countries around the world, and in 45 of the fifty U.S. states—statistics tracked by the Association of Film Commissioners International, a group whose very existence is testament to the global dissemination of the idea over the past decades. So it is almost impossible to recall how extraordinary and unprecedented the concept of the Mayor's Film Office seemed in 1966—except by recounting the almost comically difficult production conditions that prevailed in New York (and just about everywhere else) at the time.

Since the late 1940s filmmakers had been attempting to shoot features on location in the city—excited and attracted by the sense of authenticity afforded by actual locations, by the energy and vibrancy of New York's bustling urban landscape, and by the sheer visual power of the city on screen. As filmmakers such as Billy Wilder (*The Lost Weekend*, *The Seven Year Itch*), Jules Dassin (*The Naked City*), and Henry Hathaway (*The House on 92nd Street*, *Fourteen Hours*) began shooting in New York, they generated a cinematic imagery that audiences found mesmerizing, at once gritty yet filled with grandeur, intimate and human in its detail, yet capable of sweeping vistas and settings unlike anything possible on a studio lot.

But if the attractions of location shooting were obvious, so were the problems—not least due to the city itself. In 1947 (not coincidentally the year that *Naked City*, the first modern feature to be shot almost entirely in New York, was filmed in 107 locations around the five boroughs) the city's Department of Commerce and Public Events first established a small division to "advise cinema producers on the processing of applications with the police, the Borough Presidents, and other departments for location permits in filmmaking," in the words of a *New York Times* article that hinted at some of the bureaucratic complexity involved. Although the Department of Commerce issued shooting permits, those approvals had to be "endorsed" by the Police, Highway, and Traffic Departments. If wires and cables were used, the permission of the Department of Water Supply, Gas and Electricity was needed, and if park property was being used, additional permission was required from the Parks Department. Agency heads often demanded to see scripts beforehand, and would refuse filmmakers use of their facilities unless their departments were presented in a positive light.

The process, the city itself later admitted, was "complicated, vexatious, and time-consuming." Eight forms had to be filled out for each permit. Each permit was valid for one specific location, and one day;

if the company needed to move down the street for a second shot, or inclement weather delayed filming more than a few hours, new permits had to be obtained. Even a few days of shooting in the city might thus call for twenty permits, while a more ambitious production schedule could necessitate up to fifty such approvals.

It got worse from there. In order to qualify for a city permit, producers often had to satisfy an array of outlandish requirements, such as the rule that a licensed electrician—at a cost of fifty dollars a day—be present on set at all times. In fact, "about ninety different kinds of inspectors," one city official recalled, were either officially required or would simply show up on shoots, threatening to shut down the production if they were not "compensated"—i.e., paid off.

Then there were the police. Obtaining police assistance—essential to reroute traffic around a location shoot—required a trip to the local precinct, whose jurisdiction extended only to its immediate area; a shoot in multiple locations (typical of most filming) required multiple visits to different precincts, with the attendant aggravation and wear-and-tear. "You know what movie production schedules are like," Lindsay's chief-of-staff Jay Kriegel recalled, "one day I'm shooting in Washington Square, and the next day I've got to move to Times Square."

I'm going to a different precinct, I'm doing it through a different command, I've got totally different guys, nobody's talked to them, I've got to go make my own deals—whatever that means—I may have a guy who's sensitive to it, I may have a guy who's not. Each place I go, I've got to ask the precinct captain to assign cops to me. What does he get for it? It's not a priority, it has nothing to do with crime, so the fact is, it was a terrible deterrent. It also made it a really blinding experience, because you didn't know what you were going to get.

It was no secret what those "deals" often consisted of. "Oh, yes," the director Sidney Lumet later observed. "In fact we used to budget for it. You'd start shooting at seven-thirty in the morning and have to take care of all three shifts: the sergeant who'd stop by in his car, and the cops on the street." By the early 1960s, he recalls, the accepted rate for such graft was $400 for each day of shooting—no small price to pay, in 1960s dollars, for the privilege of working on the streets of the city.

But the city was not the only disincentive. By the mid-1960s, New York's motion-picture unions had earned a notorious reputation for being difficult, intransigent, and expensive. Deserved or not, these accusations came to a head in April 1965, when the veteran director Delbert Mann—who had just completed location work for an M-G-M feature called *Mister Buddwing*—delivered a stunning indictment. For three weeks, Mann had been filming around the city, including several scenes at the Washington Square campus of New York University, where the sight of a major film shoot was so unusual—the previous year only nine features had done any location work in the city—that it drew dozens of wide-eyed students from the school's department of Motion Pictures, Television and Radio—including a twenty-two year old college senior named Martin Scorsese (see page 24).

What Scorsese and his fellow students had no way of knowing was that the process had been an excruciating one for Mann, and as soon as the shooting wrapped, he let the world know it. Calling the experience "the most incredible example of non-cooperation…I have ever experienced," he vowed he would "never again come back to New York to shoot a film." Mann's words were especially damaging given his status as one of the few directors who had consistently sought to film in New York over the previous decade, shooting some or all of seven features in the city, including the landmark 1955 film *Marty*.

Mann focused his anger on his New York crew, whom he described as "uncooperative, sullen, and arrogant," eager to "take [the] company for every penny [they] could get." But the *Times* coverage of the attack—which had already appeared in the trade magazines—also mentioned, almost in passing, that the production had required thirty permits to shoot in New York at all.

That year, 1965, only eleven feature films included any location footage of New York—and only two were shot substantially in the city. Having made their dramatic reappearance two decades before, the streets of New York were in serious danger of disappearing almost entirely from American movies.

In fact, within little more than twelve months, the city would begin to explode on the screen as never before, thanks to an extraordinary series of governmental initiatives, virtually without precedent, that would soon project the image of New York in ways no one could have imagined.

To: All City Departments and Agencies…

Mayor Lindsay, a local theatre buff of long standing, has passed the word to all members of his administration to be especially helpful to movie and television producers who want to make films, or parts of films, in New York. In an executive order dated May 31st, the Mayor drastically simplified the almost Kafkaesque procedures that producers had previously had to go through to get permission to shoot on location here…. Dozens of letters have been sent to movie and TV people all over the country telling them about the changed attitude here.
THE NEW YORKER, AUGUST 13, 1966

It is fair to say that the invention of the Mayor's Office of Film, Theatre and Broadcasting—and the panoply of imaginative programs that accompanied it—would never have happened without the election in late 1965 of John Lindsay as New York City's 103rd mayor. Though his mayoralty would come to a close eight years later in a

mood of disillusion, disappointment, and unending crisis, the arrival in January 1966 of the tall, handsome, patrician young mayor—just forty-four years old at the time of his election—generated a feeling of energy and enthusiasm unseen in City Hall since the early years of Fiorello La Guardia, three decades earlier.

Among the top priorities of the new mayor was expanding film and television production. "It was a campaign commitment and a determination of mine," recalled Lindsay, who had grown close to the city's theater and film community during his years as a congressman on Manhattan's Upper East Side. "A lot of people in the entertainment and film industry who Lindsay knew," an aide observed, "and who had helped in the campaign, told him that they really wanted to live in New York but couldn't because there was not enough business. He didn't want those people leaving New York. It also really bothered him that someone would come to New York to shoot exteriors and then disappear, and not do any business here."

Another motive lay behind Lindsay's interest. Known for his elegant bearing and striking looks, the Mayor was something of a performer manqué, who enjoyed his happiest moments at the annual press club dinner, performing routines prepared for him by the songwriters Kander and Ebb. "He was a very social animal, he loved the theater, he liked being around show business people," one colleague recalled. "And with that came a love of films. He saw it had tremendous potential for New York's economy—not only to create jobs, but if it worked it would get enormous publicity."

Within weeks of his inauguration, Lindsay had selected a special assistant named Barry Gottehrer—a veteran newspaperman and former city editor at the *Herald Tribune*—to canvass the industry and come up with a package of proposals. It was an inspired choice. "Barry has had the advantage, in everything he has done in his life, of not knowing better," his former colleague Jay Kriegel has observed. "Being a reporter, someone who asked questions, very fact-laden, and very detail-oriented in asking, 'why not?' Very commonsensical." Gottehrer quickly made the rounds of the Hollywood studios and independent producers (including Ray Stark, then in pre-production for *Funny Girl*), listening to their litany of concerns and complaints, and gathering the facts for his report to the Mayor.

"I remember Barry's first report," Kriegel recalls, "I remember it because I remember how simple and powerful it was." Gottehrer made several proposals, obvious perhaps in retrospect but unheard-of at the time. First, that the city establish what he called a "one-stop system"—a single agency issuing a single permit, free of charge, good for shooting anywhere in the city, and valid for the length of the production. Second, that a single, high-profile unit of the Police Department be created to assist film crews working anywhere in the five boroughs. Third, that a special aide be appointed, working directly under the Mayor, to assist producers with problems they might encounter while filming on location. And finally, that the Mayor himself officially direct all agency heads to cooperate with film and television production in the city.

Lindsay threw his full weight behind the report, and by the end of May, with the issuance of Executive Order 10, all of Gottehrer's proposals were set in motion. The new permit process began immediately, under the hands of an efficient former receptionist named Mary Imperato—who was as impressed as anyone by the streamlined system. "I couldn't believe the ingenuity," she said. "One permit, one schedule, one signature." The movie and television police unit was soon organized, comprising a captain, four sergeants, and fifteen patrolmen. To serve as the "Mayor's Executive Coordinator of Film Making in New York," Gottehrer found a bright young woman named Joy Manhoff Flink, who had worked in production in Hollywood before relocating to New York with her husband, the writer Bill Manhoff (*The Owl and the Pussycat*). "Joy was terrific, just the ideal hire," Kriegel recalls. "She knew everybody in the industry, she had enough stature and social status to deal with people as principals, one on one—she wasn't a kid in that sense—and she was very smart about what was important, how to get things done and deal with people on both sides. She was endlessly running up against bureaucrats and red tape, and she was endlessly charming and skillful and seductive." Manhoff set up shop in a small office at 51 Chambers Street, across from City Hall. Though the conditions were hardly glamorous—it would be a year before she obtained so much as a secretary—her office soon became the crossroads for a resurgent film business in New York, and the kernel of what would become the Mayor's Office of Film, Theatre and Broadcasting.

With the film office more or less in place, Gottehrer went the extra mile, seeing if the city could use its influence to deal with what producers regarded as the second major obstacle to increasing production. "The unions were the big thing," he later observed—and to address the problem, Gottehrer scheduled a battery of meetings between labor leaders and the Mayor. It quickly became evident that the unions' difficult reputation was not unfounded. Jealously guarding what little work they had, the city's locals refused to consider any changes to their notoriously inflexible work rules and manning practices.

After a frustrating month or so, Gottehrer tried a different approach. Instead of trying to convince the unions to make concessions on the work they had, he asked them to bend their rules for the work they *didn't* have. If the city could convince a producer to shoot not just a few exteriors in New York but all, or nearly all, of a feature film—something that almost never happened—would the unions consider a special arrangement? They would be giving away nothing they already had, Gottehrer pointed out, and stood only to gain.

The ice began to break. Though they would not put specific terms in writing, a key union—Local 52, representing grips and electricians,

under the leadership of Ken Fundus—voted to cut a special deal for films made substantially in the city. Tom O'Donnell, local president of the Teamsters, agreed—and with the two powerful leaders on board, the other unions fell in line. "I don't know if they really thought it would work," Gottehrer recalls, "but Lindsay was very popular, they were both smart enough to realize it was a no-lose situation." Gottehrer's decision to involve the Mayor himself in the negotiations had helped to win over the union leaders, just as it did on the other side with producers and directors—all of whom were flattered by the attention.* "None of it would have happened without Lindsay," Gottehrer observes.

Now Manhoff's office took on a new role, as liaison between filmmakers and the unions. "She really did everything," Gottehrer recalled, "met with producers beforehand, met with union leaders to make sure the special deals really happened." "Thank God I had a good liver," Manhoff herself recalls, "there were an awful lot of meetings at Downey's and a lot of other pubs." As the first feature films—*Luv*, *Up the Down Staircase*, *Wait Until Dark*, *The Night They Raided Minsky's*, *You're a Big Boy Now*—committed to substantial production in the city, Manhoff served up another bonus, arranging to have Mayor Lindsay—with the City Hall press corps in tow—personally visit the set, to welcome the filmmakers and have his picture taken with the cast and crew (see pages 38–39). "They loved that," Manhoff recalls.

Indeed, after decades of confronting officials whose attitudes ranged from stony indifference to active hostility, moviemakers could not believe that someone in city government was actually trying to *help* them. "Mostly there was just relief that finally someone was paying attention, and seemed to care," Manhoff later recalled. Soon filmmakers were falling over themselves to tell the press how pleased they were. "If you want to know why I am so happy doing this picture in New York, ask the Mayor," said Norman Lear, the producer of *The Night They Raided Minsky's*. "I never in all my experience filming in the great cities of the world found so much help from the local authorities," the director Terence Young declared after finishing *Wait Until Dark*. Even more stunning to some was the difference the new police unit had made. "Payoffs? We didn't so much as give the cops a cup of coffee," the producer Phil Feldman exclaimed in wonderment. "About the only time [moviemakers are] delayed by a city official on the set," one newspaper reported glowingly, "is when the Mayor shows up to welcome them."

The results were astonishing—and almost instantaneous. In 1966, the number of feature films shot in part or in whole in New York leapt from 11 to 25. The production total for the first three months of 1967 equaled that for all of 1966, and by the end of the year, the number of features filmed in the city had reached 42. Over Lindsay's full two terms in office, no fewer than 366 feature films would be shot in whole or in part in New York City.

---

* To this day, the fact that the agency is called the *Mayor's* Office of Film, Theatre and Broadcasting has helped gain it the respect of Hollywood producers, who—exquisitely sensitive to questions of status—are pleased to be dealing, even implicitly, with New York's chief executive.

"For the first time," the Mayor himself later observed with evident pride, "our parks and museums, our streets and courthouses, our libraries and monuments, all these things that make New York unique, have been made available to film people."

The Most Filmic City in the World

The city of New York has helped American movies grow up.
PAULINE KAEL, 1971

In 1974, the Mayor's Office of Film, Theatre and Broadcasting made a crucial transition when a new mayor, Abraham D. Beame, succeeded John Lindsay as mayor. A relatively colorless professional politician—whose mayoralty would be all but swallowed by the growing fiscal crisis—Beame had no particular interest in the entertainment industry, but the value of the Mayor's Film Office had become so evident that he had no choice but to continue his predecessor's efforts. After a few months of dithering, Beame appointed as the office's director a former producer named Walter Wood, who declared that despite its widening social and economic troubles, "New York is the most filmic city in the world. You can't point your camera at anything in this city and come up with something dull and uninteresting. You can film anything in one or another of the five boroughs."

By that time, it was becoming obvious that the explosion in location shooting that the Mayor's Office had helped bring forth was having far wider cultural and artistic repercussions than the narrow (if undoubtedly worthy) economic and employment goals that had driven its founding. Since the late 1960s, an extraordinary new chapter in American filmmaking had opened—one that was centered, to a remarkable degree, on the streets and sidewalks of New York.

By then, the influence of the New Wave—as well as the more general desire to work in actual locations—was being felt all around the world, except perhaps in the big Hollywood studios, where veteran directors and production chiefs clung fiercely to old familiar ways. But a new crop of young American filmmakers was just then rising to challenge the establishment, and for many of them, the same impulse to make new kinds of films—more authentic, more immediate, more open to the casual, improvised nature of real life—would carry them, like the French, out of the studio and into the streets of the city. That city, of course, would not be Paris, but its closest American equivalent: New York.

In the early and mid-1970s, as part of a creative outpouring that critics would later suggest was America's decade-later counterpart to the New Wave, a cadre of young directors would use the new freedom to shoot on location in New York—and the white-hot intensity, in those same years, of the city's, racial, economic and urban tensions—as the instrument for a series of films as provocative and innovative as any being produced in the world. Brilliant young filmmakers such as Martin Scorsese (*Mean Streets*, *Taxi Driver*),

William Friedkin (*The French Connection*), Hal Ashby (*The Landlord*), Brian de Palma (*Greetings*), Alan Pakula (*Klute*), and Francis Ford Coppola (*You're a Big Boy Now*, *The Godfather*, and *The Godfather, Part II*) would help shift the use of location shooting—and New York itself—from the fringe to the mainstream of American movies, an effort reinforced by the work of several other major figures whose personal background and artistic impulses drew them time and again to the city. The New York–based director Sidney Lumet, already legendary for his groundbreaking location films of the 1960s, would cement his reputation during the decade with a string of four extraordinary films—*Serpico*, *Dog Day Afternoon*, *Network*, *Prince of the City*—that drew directly on the ethnic and cultural complexities of the city. Paul Mazursky, a native New Yorker who had moved to Hollywood years before, returned to his hometown to create two sharply etched portraits—both filmed almost entirely on location—of historic and contemporary New York: *Next Stop, Greenwich Village* and *An Unmarried Woman*. And of course, the 1970s saw the rise of the Brooklyn-born writer and filmmaker Woody Allen, whose location-shot romantic comedies (*Annie Hall*, *Manhattan*, and a few years later, *Hannah and Her Sisters*, among many others) would literally define a certain vision of New York—and New Yorkers—for audiences around the world. But the lure of the city would also draw filmmakers from farther afield, including Roman Polanski (*Rosemary's Baby*), John Schlesinger (*Midnight Cowboy*), Milos Forman (*Hair*), and Alan Parker (*Fame*)—each of whom, looking at the urban landscape with the fresh eyes of an outsider, would create some of the most memorable film moments of the era.

In retrospect, the location-shot New York films of this era owed much of their distinctive look and feel to an extraordinary confluence of trends and influences, a product of the city's unusual, highly variegated film scene. Unlike Los Angeles, where the studios utterly dominated the production landscape, New York's smaller, scrappier feature industry stood in fertile proximity to several other, equally vital moviemaking traditions. There was the heritage of gifted documentary filmmakers—Helen Levitt, Rudy Burckhardt, Shirley Clarke—who for decades had employed silent 16mm cameras and available light to create a series of short, unforgettable portraits of New York's urban life and landscape. There was the cadre of the city's younger documentary practitioners—Donn Pennebaker, Ricky Leacock, Robert Drew, Albert and David Maysles—who in the late 1950s had pushed the technology of 16mm cameras to incorporate synchronized sound, allowing them to capture the sights and sounds of ordinary life—on the street, in rooms, just about anywhere—as it was taking place. At the other end of the spectrum, there was the bustling commercial industry, which in sheer economic terms represented by far the largest component of the city's film business. In the mid-1960s, no fewer than 85 percent of all U.S. television commercials were produced in New York City, the undisputed capital (then as now) of the nation's advertising industry. Thanks to the advent of the celebrated "creative revolution" in American advertising in those same years, the thirty-second television spot arguably became the most innovative film production medium in the world, a well-financed laboratory in which young cinematographers like Adam Holender, Owen Roizman, and Gordon Willis could experiment with new lenses and camera equipment, unusual film stocks and processing techniques, and a host of fresh production ideas—including the extensive use of lightweight cameras for location shooting, and the earliest use of video equipment, tapped off the camera lens, to provide instant playback (an innovation that, in taking much of the guesswork out of exposure, focus, and camera movement, allowed filmmakers to take greater chances in the unpredictable conditions that so often accompanied location work).

One way or another, all of these influences would find their way into the location-shot movies of the late 1960s and 1970s, as the city's feature moviemakers eagerly adopted the techniques and equipment of documentaries, or, in some cases, graduated from doing commercial work to features—as was the case with Holender, Roizman, and Willis, who transferred their daring, experimental approach from the commercial arena to the extraordinary photography of *Midnight Cowboy*, *The French Connection*, and *Manhattan*, respectively.

As was obvious from all the features of this era, the spirit of cross-fertilization extended far beyond the world of film production itself, spilling over to the world of live theater—where, thanks to the presence of Broadway and off-Broadway, the city reigned supreme. "In New York the last thing you ever have to worry about is actors," the director Sidney Lumet once observed. "You can stand on any corner, turn around five times and cast the picture. The talent is never-ending." As the *New York Times* observed in 1981, the rise of location shooting in New York literally changed the face of American film performance:

> The urban-oriented, street-smart films of Woody Allen, Martin Scorsese, Paul Mazursky, Sidney Lumet, and the like demanded a gritty "realness" and an ethnic vitality not often found in Hollywood's gorgeously manufactured land of make-believe. Films shot on location in Manhattan also provided access to the thousands of fine New York actors whose training in the theater gave them an essential advantage over California actors who ply their trade under less rigorous discipline on television. Of course, Hollywood casting directors have always understood the value of stage experience and routinely visit New York to see actors, even casting whole films here, but in general they're handicapped by having to judge actors on the basis of a quick meeting in a hotel suite, while New York casting directors intimate with the theater scene will know first-hand the range of an actor's capabilities.... With their emphasis on creating an individualized, even idiosyncratic look, films like Mr. Allen's *Manhattan*, Mr. Mazursky's *An Unmarried Woman*, and Mr. Scorsese's *Raging Bull* use actors very differently than big-budget, star-studded Hollywood movies such as *The Four Seasons* or *California Suite* do. These directors preferred to find specific, not necessarily familiar faces to represent the particular world of a film; they wanted individual performances rather than the interaction of "types."

Made in New York

> The boom means many things to many people. In a historic sense, it marks a renaissance for a city where the art of movie-making once flourished, then fled. For the City of New York, beset with economic woes of wide notoriety and harrowing import, it means an infusion of money measured in the millions of dollars and the exhilarating payoff of long and arduous efforts to entice movie-makers to return; for its workmen, artisans, and artists—many of whom are New Yorkers by fierce and unyielding choice—it means an opportunity to work at a trade they cherish in a city they love.
> LAWRENCE VAN GELDER, *NEW YORK TIMES*, 1980

By the 1980s, the thrilling early explosion in location filming had settled into a somewhat steadier rhythm, as a stream of logistical and technological advances substantially routinized the once-unpredictable process of shooting on the city's streets. An entire industry now arose to create what were, in effect, movie studios on wheels—fleets of vehicles that could bring to any corner of the city an array of resources scarcely less complex or advanced than that of a Hollywood sound stage—cameras, lights, cranes, sound, wardrobe, makeup, props, sanitary facilities and "craft services" (as the industry terms food service for cast and crew). As the number of films shot in the city each year soared past a hundred—then approached two hundred—the scale and ambition of location work grew ever larger, until the presence of film crews had become a familiar element in the city's landscape—thrilling tourists and many residents while frustrating many others, who exercised their inalienable rights as New Yorkers to complain loudly about an activity that almost anywhere else in the world would evoke a measure of excitement and awe. (To be fair, the residents of especially picturesque parts of the city did suffer the disruption of film and TV productions far more than others, leading the Mayor's Office to sometimes declare a temporary "hold" on certain streets and neighborhoods.)

By the end of the 1980s, the outlines of another trend had begun to emerge. The resurgence in location filming two decades earlier had given rise over the intervening years to an indigenous filmmaking culture in New York, as numbers of aspiring young moviemakers looked not to Southern California's well-established film schools (USC and UCLA) but to New York University, whose highly regarded film production program was grounded largely in location technique. Following in the footsteps of Martin Scorsese, who had studied and taught at the school in the 1960s, NYU graduates such as Spike Lee, Jim Jarmusch, and Susan Seidelman created a series of personally expressive feature films (*She's Gotta Have It*, *Stranger Than Paradise*, *Smithereens*) that were rooted intimately in the city and relied extensively—for both artistic and economic reasons—on location shooting around New York. Together with several others, they also helped give rise to a new "independent" film industry, centered in New York, that would extend the innovations of the 1970s to create a distinct alternative to conventional Hollywood product—one that soon became so successful, financially as well as artistically, that the studios sought to bring its production and distribution companies into their own fold.

Though the early 1990s saw a brief but devastating setback—when the studios sought to curb rising labor costs by way of a nine-month boycott on all production in New York—by the middle of the decade the industry had rebounded into one of its greatest periods of growth. Almost every sector of the business expanded, from big-budget studio films—which grew ever more ambitious in the scale of their location shooting—to smaller independent features, whose tiny, dedicated crews could be found working in every corner of the city. A new generation of forward-thinking union leaders and members, meanwhile, were fast overturning labor's old reputation for inflexibility. Even those parts of the industry which had lagged for years now burst into action, as the rise of cable network television made New York the center for a new kind of sophisticated episodic series (*Sex and the City*, *The Sopranos*), and the renovation of two sprawling studio complexes in western Queens (Kaufman Astoria and Silvercup, both of which had been expanding since the 1980s) gave the city the large-scale, state-of-the-art sound stages it had always lacked.

Almost none of this would have been possible, of course, without the continuing efforts of the Mayor's Office (reinforced after 1979 by the Governor's Office for Motion Picture and Television Development, which could help to deliver a rich inventory of state-run locations, from the subway system and Grand Central to the far-flung facilities of the Port Authority, including tunnels, bridges, airports, and the twin towers of the World Trade Center). Despite chronic underfunding and rising competition from other states and municipalities (which had belatedly realized what Lindsay's team had seen years before) the small, hardworking staff of the Mayor's Office managed to preserve a unique reputation within the industry for their energy and effectiveness: running interference with other city agencies, helping to identify and secure locations, and allowing filmmakers to work in places they could not have dreamed of a few years before—from the Brooklyn Bridge (*Hudson Hawk* and *Stay*) to a night scene of Times Square filled with extras (*Last Action Hero*) and, even more remarkably, a day scene of Times Square, entirely empty (*Vanilla Sky*). As the scope and ambition of location shoots continued to expand, ever larger responsibility fell on the Police Department's Movie and TV Unit, which had doubled in size by the late 1990s to five senior officers and thirty patrolmen. In retrospect, many observers felt that it was the creation of this specialized unit, even more than the streamlined permit process, that marked the greatest of New York's 1960s innovations. "Once you get the permitting done," Jay Kriegel has observed, "the front line of making the city accessible is really the cops, and the notion of a senior [police officer] who's responsive and cares and it's his job, and he sees it as a legitimate function, who'll go wherever [the film company] is going, and [makes sure] that the same guys are going to stay with [the production], that, I think, is what makes the city welcoming and effective as a place to film more than anything else."

As the new century began, however, a triple blow threatened to undo much of the progress of the previous three and a half decades. First, the combination of a favorable currency exchange rate and a new tax credit made it enormously profitable to "cheat" New York by shooting in Canada. Second, the city's economy, like that of the country as a whole, began taking a dramatic down-turn in the middle of 2001. And then, of course, came September 11, which, despite the heartfelt efforts of West Coast producers (including many former New Yorkers), inevitably took its toll on production in the city. In the summer of 2002, when newly elected Mayor Michael R. Bloomberg—New York's first chief executive to come from the world of media and broadcasting—appointed one of his former managers, Katherine Oliver, as the commissioner of the Mayor's Office, the glorious heritage of New York filmmaking faced a deeply uncertain future. "When I went out to Los Angeles in the fall of 2002 to meet with all of the studio heads and the heads of production," she recalled, "many of them told me that when they got a script with New York in it, they would send it back and say 'change the city.' Or we were having films that were coming here for a day or two and then running to Canada and faking New York"—the same phenomenon that had so angered John Lindsay, nearly forty years before.

In a burst of activity reminiscent of the agency's founding, Oliver quickly put in place a series of short-term initiatives, while laying plans for larger changes to come. Astonished to discover in 2002 that the office was still processing permits by hand, using electric typewriters—a process that could take anywhere from three hours to three days—she reassigned staff, put the permits online, and cut the approval time to fifteen or twenty minutes. She created a "concierge" desk, hiring a former locations manager—whose business it was to know every location in the city—to encourage producers to work in the city by literally finding them places to shoot. She helped arrange for a directive from Mayor Bloomberg restating what Lindsay had declared in 1966: that all city agencies must cooperate with the Mayor's Film Office, because movie and television production means big business for New York. And she began a marketing campaign to remind the industry of the essential benefits established by Mayor Lindsay decades earlier, and still unmatched by any other city in the world: free permits, free police, free parking, and free use of parks and city buildings.

At the same time, a long-term strategy began to take shape, centered on an ambitious tax credit that would level the playing field with Canada. In January 2005, Mayor Bloomberg signed a historic program into law, providing a 5 percent tax credit on qualified expenses for feature films and television series produced substantially in the city, to augment the state's 10 percent tax credit. To help producers calculate the savings, Oliver added a business development expert to the concierge desk, then watched as the credit, in her words, "changed the nature of the business." The $50 million allocated by the city for four years was exhausted in just fourteen months—bringing in $650 million in new business and six thousand new jobs along the way. The tax credit was then expanded in July 2006 to encompass $30 million from the city through 2011, complementing the State's initiative to expand its annual offering to $60 million through that time period. Meanwhile the second part of Oliver's long-term strategy got underway, a "Made in NY" marketing credit that ingeniously leveraged city assets—free outdoor media on bus shelters and phone kiosks, for example—to help promote film and TV projects that were actually produced in the five boroughs. "There were far too many projects that were faking New York," Oliver observes, "and we wanted to tell the public, you should be looking out for the difference…the 'Made in NY' logo is our Good Housekeeping seal; only the projects that qualify get to display it."

To be sure, larger forces were aligning in the city's favor, from a shift in the exchange rate between the U.S. and Canadian dollar to the opening in 2004 of a third major production facility in New York City: the Steiner Studios at the Brooklyn Navy Yard, which included the largest purpose-built sound stage east of Hollywood, a 100,000-square-foot behemoth created with design and technical assistance from Sony Entertainment. At the same time, a dramatic increase in tourism to the city—a record 43 million visitors in 2005—helped to drive up theater attendance on Broadway (whose economic well-being is also a mandate of the Mayor's Office).

Whatever the precise mix of causes, by the middle of the decade New York's entertainment industry—and especially film and television production—had entered a period of growth unlike anything in its history. The number of location shooting days in the city (the most accurate measure of production activity), which had risen steadily across the 1990s but dipped significantly in the wake of 9/11, began rising steeply again and by 2004 had exceeded its previous peak in 1998. As the impact of the tax credit and other changes began to take hold, however, the amount of location shooting in the city simply exploded, rising 35 percent in 2005 to reach an unheard-of total of 31,570 days. By 2006 the Mayor's Office was churning out well over a hundred permits a day, and an agency that had begun forty years earlier with a three-page document and two desks had become the cornerstone of a five-billion-dollar-a-year industry, employing over a hundred thousand New Yorkers.

All of this economic activity and increased employment has been a crucial boon to the city, of course, especially as New York completes a long and often painful transition from its industrial past to its information-based future (film and television production, both a blue-collar industry and a creative pursuit, has, significantly, a foot in both worlds). But for all its economic benefits, it is in the end the *in*tangible value of this extraordinary filmmaking heritage—its continuing power to convert the daily reality of the city into a magical, transcendent realm, capturing the hearts and minds of

millions around the world—that remains the Mayor's Office's greatest gift to New York, sustaining the city's special place in the contemporary imagination, and preserving it—in all its complexity, beauty, tension, and excitement—for countless generations to come.

A Brief Note on Structure

New York, like all cities, exists in both space and time. In celebrating the extraordinary heritage of location filming in New York over the past four decades, *Scenes from the City* offers a survey shaped by chronology as well as geography—two vectors that have helped give the book its unusual, overlapping structure.

The book's primary framework is chronological, proceeding decade by decade from the mid-1960s through the present. Each section covers its ten-year period by opening with some of the best-remembered location films of that era and some of the distinctive landmarks found in those films, and closes with a selection of evocative filmic New York "moments" from that same ten years. (A final section covers all four decades of location shooting for television, including episodic series, talk shows, music videos, commercials, and children's programming.)

Set within this larger structure are a variety of subjects that transcend chronology. At more or less regular intervals, *Scenes from the City* touches down to explore an area of the city in greater detail, through a selective survey of some of those districts and neighborhoods—from Coney Island to SoHo, Central Park to the Bronx, Greenwich Village to the Upper West Side—that have most frequently, and vividly, captured the attention of filmmakers working on location.

Other, similarly "timeless" sections look at specific aspects of shooting on location, from the construction of ambitious, backlot-type sets on actual city streets, to the transformation of ordinary New York blocks for period films or fantasies, to the adaptation of familiar cinematic devices, such as chases or stunts, to the unusual needs and possibilities of the city's dense urban landscape. And still others explore the "state of the art" of location shooting, from the little-known but critical role of the still photographer (whose work comprises most of the images in the book itself) to the dramatic evolution—technical, logistical, and artistic—of location filmmaking itself. It is perhaps these images, in the end, that take us furthest into the heart of the entire astonishing enterprise: bringing cameras, equipment, and the world's most famous performers onto the streets of one of the biggest, fastest moving, and most restless cities on earth.

THE CITY HAS BECOME THE GREAT STUDIO…
A CONVERSATION WITH MARTIN SCORSESE

Martin Scorsese, on the set of *Goodfellas* (1990), in Queens, New York.

Interview conducted on 4/10/2006 by James Sanders
at Mr. Scorsese's offices in Manhattan

What was your first experience with location shooting in New York?

The first time I saw a film being shot, it was a night scene of [the TV series] "Naked City," and they came to my neighborhood, Elizabeth and Houston Streets. This was the late '50s, and it was the first time I saw anything like that in my life. I must have been sixteen or seventeen, and it was up by a little park on the north side of Houston—I don't know if that park is there now, probably isn't, I think there's a building there now. [In those days] no one came into that neighborhood, it was a wonderful community of people, Italian-Americans, Italians from different parts of Italy, but at the same time it was also kind of a closed neighborhood in the sense of, you know, organized crime figures and that sort of thing, and to a certain extent it was a little dangerous in the streets, you had the rise of the "Blackboard Jungle," juvenile delinquents, young bloods having fights with other young bloods in the streets, so that no one came to that neighborhood from the outside, it was *locked*. So here we were, in the middle of the nighttime, they're shooting there, they're making rain, and there's one guy on the ground in a raincoat, and the other guy's standing over him and he has a *harpoon* aimed at him, and the other guy's begging for his life. And of course the kids in my neighborhood started making noise, and they had to be taken away, they were really unfriendly. But I couldn't quite believe it, it looked… the actors had a *strength* to them. The harpoon thing was absurd, of course, but making rain was kind of interesting to me and the next location filming I saw, also "Naked City," they shot in a very, very photogenic location—certainly one of the ten most photogenic locations in New York: Jersey Street, right off of Mulberry, towards old St. Patrick's Church; those two blocks are just incredible, and that alley has a long history going back to the period of *Gangs of New York*. Those are the only two times I saw films being made [as a teenager], and they were both "Naked City."

You've said you spent much of your childhood in the city watching films, in movie houses like the Loew's Commodore on East 6th Street, and on television. Given your own later interest as a filmmaker in working on location, how did you respond to those landmark early features shot in and around New York, such as On the Waterfront *(1954) and* Force Of Evil *(1948)?*

Those early location films were important to us. *Waterfront* was a key film. The fact that it was in Hoboken didn't matter. There was something about the authenticity of the streets, the cobblestones, the faces, the costumes, that we appropriated as being Lower East Side, Italian American. Okay, towards the West Side, the docks, we'll go that far (laughs). That was literally like, I never thought I'd see that kind of thing on the screen. *Force of Evil* was earlier and was another key film, the opening sequence of *Wall Street* alone—Wall Street empty—is glorious, as glorious as the ending of *Manhattan* by Woody Allen, of course in a different way—a darker way (*laughs*).

What I find impressive about Force of Evil *is that it actually contains very few location shots, only five or six in all, but they are arranged to trace a coherent geography, a descent that renders in physical terms the moral and emotional journey of the rackets lawyer played by John Garfield—from the rarefied heights of a Wall Street skyscraper, to the "everyday" level of the streets, and then still further down, to the terrible discovery of his brother's body, washed up in the river.*

Yes, with the repetition of his voice-over dialogue: "I went down and down there…to find my brother." It's one of the most moving films and one of the most beautiful films ever made. They call it a *noir*. I guess it is a *noir*, but of course it's more than that, for many different reasons—the philosophy of it is stronger. I love *Force of Evil* so much; it made such a major impact on my life. And one of the key things in watching that film was identifying the places where it was shot, those five or six location scenes. How can I put it? When we saw those locations, that made it ours, this happened to *us* and it happened right here. And there's the proof. Okay, it wasn't with double-breasted suits and it wasn't with telephones with people with fancy lawyers, but it happens to us every day.

Another early influence must have been Sidney Lumet, who had started his extraordinary string of New York-shot films by the late 1950s.

Oh, he's absolutely key. That's the other thing too, in the '50s, Lumet's films. I mean the first time I saw something that actually played out the democratic process, or process of what America could be, was *12 Angry Men* [1957]. And it was Lumet and his energy and style, I think, and of course Boris Kaufman's photography, and the screenplay was quite something, originally from TV, it was that whole period when television plays were being turned into films….

Like Marty *in 1955…*

Marty is a good depiction of New York, it had that "slice-of-life" feel because it's black and white, but again it's a very accurate depiction of the decent people of Italian-American descent, the ones who are not involved with crime…I shouldn't use the word "decent," let's say instead, the majority of Italian Americans, because some people who make mistakes are decent, that's what I've learned.

You had just graduated from Washington Square College of New York University—and were just starting your career as a filmmaker—when the Mayor's Office of Film, Theatre and Broadcasting was started in 1966. Can you recall what it was like in the years just before and after the creation of the Mayor's Office?

The big deal prior to that was that any film coming to New York to shoot was a big event. The other day *Mister Buddwing* was on television, filmed in 1965, Delbert Mann directing, with a number of scenes shot down at [NYU's] Washington Square College at the Main Building. I was there when they were shooting it. We were all amazed, of course, by the giant lights that were being used, and everything else. And if you look at them today, the images of those films give you an instant recall on what it was like to walk on the streets of New York at that time. The streets were somehow—you could see in *Mister Buddwing* and other films shot around that time—had a more austere feel to them, the cars were somewhat bigger, the men wore hats, and raincoats. So it feels comforting to see it if you lived through it, and reminds us of being film students at Washington Square College.

By then you had begun to make your own short 16mm films around the city, which was something of a tradition at NYU even then and has become a famous aspect of the program in the decades since. What was it like trying to shoot films around the streets of New York as a student?

At that time, in the early '60s, it was difficult—this is a city, after all, you can't put a camera out in the first lane of traffic and then divert traffic. Especially if you're a bunch of kids who don't even know how to use the camera that well, you know what I'm talking about? When we would go to shoot those films in '63 to '65, New York was not at all used to films being shot on the street, so the easiest answer we gave everybody asking, "what are you shooting, what are you doing?" was "Naked City," because that was the only thing people were used to. They'd say "absolutely," and leave us alone.

You've described the incredible range of influences that came together for you and your fellow film students in New York in the late 1950s and early 1960s, from the work of local independent filmmakers to international movements like the French and Italian New Waves. Whatever their differences, all of these trends seem linked by the desire to move away from traditional, studio-bound filmmaking and toward location-based shooting in real settings—which was still a revolutionary idea, at least in many quarters.

A lot had to do with the breakup of the studio system. When the system broke, and cameras were brought outside of the studio— cameras had been brought outside of the studio before, in the 1920s to a certain extent, but not like this, not like the influence from Italian neorealism—cameras were really outside the studios now. And on top of that, cameras by the late '50s became lighter and faster, and then suddenly there was a breakthrough in narrative. And that had to do with Kazan, with the films he made in New York [*On the Waterfront, A Face in the Crowd, America, America*] making him, in effect, I think, the first independent filmmaker; with Kubrick becoming independent out of New York; and also with Allen Baron, who did a film in 1961 called *Blast of Silence*, which nobody seems to remember now—a very interesting film shot in the city—and with Shirley Clarke, of course, who started with *The Connection* [1962], but then the key one was *The Cool World* [1964]. And by that time, also in the late '50s, early '60s you had the experimental, avant-garde cinema coming out of New York in 16mm and 8mm; there was, of course, some in Los Angeles and San Francisco and Chicago, but it was mainly in New York, I think. And *Film Culture* magazine being such an important force in the New Cinema, which broke all ties with the studio-bound film, and was inspired by not only Italian neorealism, but French and Italian New Wave in the late '50s and early '60s. So that by the time we hit NYU, suddenly there were films being made—from *Le Beau Serge* [1958] by Claude Chabrol to Godard and Truffaut—and then Fellini's films, Bertolucci's *Before the Revolution* [1964], Antonioni, and so many others. But the real power was the ability to go into an ordinary room and be able to shoot, because the cameras had come down in size, become a little more flexible, with the crystal-sync motor, and at the same time you had something happening with documentary cinema, or non-fiction cinema, and that's Donn Pennebaker, Ricky Leacock, and of course the Maysles brothers.

It seems as if your professors at NYU firmly pointed you toward these location-based trends, and not the traditional Hollywood studio approach.

At Washington Square College, our teacher Haig Manoogian was never one to emphasize feature filmmaking of the kind that came out of Hollywood. He hated that. He used to say, if you bring me a script and there's a gun in it, I'm throwing you out. He didn't realize that you could still have a gun and it could still be truthful. What he meant was, he didn't want anybody to go for genre filmmaking, that's Hollywood. So his main touchstones were Italian neorealism, lots of wonderful films from the '20s from Germany and America, and of course, documentary filmmaking, Leo Hurwitz and Robert Flaherty, and James Agee and Helen Levitt's *In the Street*, that's the kind of films he thought we should be making. When Pennebaker, Leacock and the Maysles came together in the late '50s, this just fit perfectly into the NYU way of thinking about filmmaking, because there was no such thing as any of us students making a feature film in Hollywood, it was out of the question. In fact by that time, we felt as students that we'd just make films, in other words you don't go to Hollywood, because now it's valid in New York, it's valid on the East Coast.

You've also noted how important an influence you found John Cassavetes' independently produced 1959 feature, Shadows, which he shot with a 16mm camera on actual locations all around New York.

That was the gauntlet that was thrown down to every film student, every film lover, who felt they could make a film but said, "Oh I don't have enough money, I don't have this, I don't have that." And we said, Oh yeah? Take a look at this. If you have something to say you'll find a way to get a camera, even if you've got to steal it. And in New York you could do that, there were ways, there were camera houses, people took some equipment out—no, sorry, "borrowed" it—and maybe it was brought back, who knows? You fought over certain things. You'd steal things from construction sites to help build sets. You have to do it!

It was certainly a very different approach than that followed by the two professional film programs in Southern California, at USC and UCLA, the traditional "feeder" schools to the studio system in Hollywood.

For a long period of time, the California schools, USC and UCLA, would ridicule student films from Washington Square College, because they would say, you can always tell an NYU film, it's always two kids talking and walking in Washington Square Park. But then that changed! That changed! (*Laughs*) After I left in 1965, then the NYU School of the Arts was formed, then [by the 1980s] you got Spike Lee. But that was after my time.

It changed, one might argue, largely because of the extraordinary impact on young New York filmmakers of your own career, especially after you made the leap to writing and directing your own feature films, starting with Who's That Knocking at My Door *in 1967. In so many ways, that film seems a direct outgrowth of the kind of street-based short films you had been making at NYU.*

Yes, Haig Manoogian, my professor, eventually became one of my producers, got some money, the whole thing was finally made for $35,000 altogether, my father helped a little, and that was just shot in New York—we didn't know what else to do!

It was your next New York-set feature, Mean Streets *(1973), that seemed to mark a decisive shift away from the traditional NYU style of moviemaking—the earnest, black-and-white films of "lonely streets and sullen bedrooms," in David Denby's words—and toward a new approach toward filming the city, one that for all its darkness, frankly acknowledged what Denby called the "voluptuous pleasures of the neighborhood."*

That's a good way of putting what we felt when we saw "Naked City" being made there, when I said nobody came to the neighborhood. *We* felt a voluptuousness of a way of life in a little world that was impenetrable, particularly because a lot of people didn't want their faces on camera, quite honestly. That all changed when *Godfather* came in later and they paid a lot of money, and people saw there was money to be made. But I could hardly shoot *Mean Streets* and *Who's That Knocking*, even though I was a neighborhood kid. My father had to pay off a lot of people. Two hundred dollars here, a hundred dollars there, which caused a lot of bad blood between people.

It is striking that audiences often regard features shot on location, particularly those in black and white, as more "real" than Technicolor, studio-shot films—though both, of course, are entirely fictional constructions, in which nearly everything has been carefully arranged beforehand. In the end, I suppose, that sense of veracity associated with location shooting and black-and-white film is a kind of hand-me-down from documentaries…

…It's a hand-me-down from newsreels! But that's going to change, I think, because what's "real" now? Color video. And so all of a sudden black and white is the past, and stylized. When we did *Raging Bull* [1980], we did black and white for a number of reasons, the least of which was period. I said it would help a little bit with the period, because I wanted it to look like the old pictures on the front page of the *Daily News*, Weegee, that sort of thing. But my first impulse was to say I'll be damned if I'm going to design this thing in color, and then the color will fade in five years—on the prints, there was no video at the time. In fact, the associate producer of the film, Gene Kirkwood, leaned in one day long before we started shooting and said, "Remember, *Sweet Smell of Success*." And I said, "Of course," and I felt completely confident, 'cause I thought of New York in my mind in black and white. Of course in my world I didn't go to the "21" Club, but we did go to the Copacabana from time to time, and the interior of that, in my mind, was black and white. That uptown New York, Broadway, and the side streets, and people waiting for the reviews, sometimes I'd see them—all black and white. It was dark at night, there was some light, there were some lightbulbs, and car headlights, but people were wearing dark coats and hats. It was black and white!

I've long thought that New York in the 1950s actually was different, more of a Nordic place, like a northern European city—more formal, more Anglo-Saxon, more of an indoor culture than today's New York, which, with its sidewalk cafes and street festivals and multicultural population, somehow feels more Mediterranean in spirit.

Right, right! More colorful, multicultural. There were a lot of problems, for example, when the Hispanics or Puerto Ricans were moving into the Italian area, one of the things the Italians complained about— the old-time Italians—complained they were painting the walls turquoise. It wasn't the right color. These Italians—you'd think they were Mediterranean, but in the meantime they're always wearing black, they're always in dark rooms.

Another way to look at Mean Streets *is as part of the extraordinary tradition of films set in the crowded tenement districts of New York— a lineage that goes all the way back to 1931's* Street Scene, *which was perhaps the first to suggest that for all their economic troubles, from a dramatic point of view tenement districts might be among the best places to set a movie, because no one wants to stay inside the buildings, everyone comes out in the street and interacts.*

Well, *Street Scene* was a very important film to us, because of the life of the people in the tenements, and how it was all brought out to the front stoop, particularly in the summertime with the windows open. In my building, 253 Elizabeth Street, which is still there, there were eight apartments, four floors, and the doors would be open and if you were friendly with the neighbors the evening was spent all together. If there was a party, if there was an argument, this all came together, people sleeping on fire escapes….People tend to think of it as colorful, but it really wasn't that colorful. It was at times extraordinary, wonderful in its own way, but you tended to want to get away from each other, because you're on top of each other all the time, and you add to that the extraordinary heat, and it wasn't so charming.

I suppose you could say that in your own upbringing and your portrayal in Mean Streets *you caught the very tail end of that way of life…*

I caught the last tail of that, enough to give you a real strong impression. So yes, it was street life, and the people in the neighborhood knew everything—they knew *everything*—within the space of two or three buildings, so all this fell out into the streets. *Mean Streets* has some of that, but it also had a lot of the life really going on—the adolescent or young adult life of the boys—really going on in after-hour joints in the backs of tenements: hidden, always underground.

There's that extraordinary sense in Mean Streets *of Little Italy being a place of intimate secrets, of "rooms within rooms"—especially in the scene of Harvey Keitel and Amy Robinson's conversation in a rear yard that almost looks like something out of Naples…*

That's on Mulberry Street, that's the building right across from Jersey Street, when you go out the backdoor under the main staircase, there's a little staircase made of iron and then you're in the backyard. The backyards were great, you could hide in the backyards, you could play hide-and-seek, you could play baseball—though I didn't play baseball—you did a lot in the backyard that people didn't catch in the window, also you had privacy under those stairwells and those hallways. That's why I shot that scene in New York, 'cause we couldn't find hallways like that in Los Angeles—and those were the same hallways, too, in the '50s, where kids would sing doo-wop. The hallway and the tiled floor. And that little area you saw with Amy and Harvey, that's literally still there, just outside the back door of that building.

When we get to Taxi Driver *(1976), the location shooting of New York takes on a completely different dimension, less a portrait of an actual city than of what the great critic Robert Warshow called "that sad and dangerous city of the imagination."*

Yes, [*pointing to head*]…it's in here.

You might say that the city in Taxi Driver *is a kind of instrument, a way to make visible what otherwise would be invisible.*

Absolutely, and the proof of that is Schrader's script….He comes from the Midwest, and he set it in New York, and when we were trying to make the film we couldn't get the money to do it, we thought about setting it in Los Angeles or San Francisco, and he thought about it for quite a while and said no, New York is the place, because the taxicabs, there's a specific way of life, there's a specific situation that they're in, there's a world in New York—particularly if you're driving at night—that's unmatched in any other part of the world. Maybe in London or Paris, but in terms of America, there's nothing like that, for better or for worse.

As a caution against reading too much documentary-like "truth" into feature films, I like to point out that Taxi Driver *and* Annie Hall—*two of the most wildly differing portraits of New York ever put on film— are in fact almost contemporary. They were shot within ten months of each other—yours in late summer of 1975 and Woody Allen's in the early summer of 1976.*

Really? See, Woody Allen has a much healthier feel about the city! He's an intellectual. He's great. *Manhattan* is one of my favorite films, the ending of *Manhattan* is one of the greatest ever put on film. I don't know…it's like the first time I tried to read *The New Yorker,* I didn't understand it. You know, I come from a culture where there was no reading, or at least in my particular household there was no reading. My parents were not educated, there were no books in the house—I brought the first ones in—and it's taken me years to learn how to read a book, really. And my culture was primarily visual, through films on television, and the iconography of the church, and different ethnic neighborhoods, the visuals of going between Jewish neighborhoods, and then the Ukrainian area—where I had to go through to get to the Tompkins Square Park library—and all of that. And, of course, cinema, movies.

And you feel Woody Allen has a more writerly background?

Absolutely, his background was just more book-friendly. There was just no tradition of reading from my parents, there just wasn't. Ultimately that cut me off a lot from some of the greater things in life, really. But for a long period of time I felt that the people in Woody Allen's films were as alien to me as, you know, people in southern India or somewhere, where, yes, I'd like to learn about Hinduism, and I'd go and learn about it but it would be something I would have to acquire, to learn. And ultimately, over the years, I got as close as possible to that literary culture to know that I don't know enough about it—and that I'll never catch up, either, and let's just be happy with what I have and do what I do, and still read for pleasure, and if that means reading *The New Yorker* from time to time for pleasure, that's good. But I find his work remarkable, like the scene in *Manhattan* where Diane Keaton's just reciting names of artists, and he goes, you just crossed off half of Western civilization. You can not beat this stuff! You can't beat it!

Of course, there are plenty of superb and powerful images in his films as well…

Oh, sure, by the time he got to *Annie Hall* he worked up the visual style, you could see from his earlier films—*Sleeper, Bananas*—he was struggling a bit and then of course *Love and Death* was close, in terms of visual style, and finally, bang, he hits it with *Annie Hall*, and since then, there's this Chekhovian-like palette of characters, New York characters, New York intellectuals, just wonderful. It's something that took me time to acquire, it doesn't mean I didn't like it when I first saw it, but it's alien to me. My New York is very different.

Years ago, Allen received a certain amount of criticism for presenting what seemed like an urban fantasyland, a city with little or no crime. I wonder if it's not more his city that we live in today–certainly very different from the vision of New York you've presented over the years!

To this day, I do not go into Central Park. I grew up in an area that was very tough, the Bowery was scary for seven or eight year-old kids, it was terrifying, and we always grew up with fear. It doesn't mean you have to be afraid in this city, but my sense is that you have to be aware, and you have to be cautious. In the Woody Allen world, that's completely overlooked—and they're fine! They're fine! [*Laughs*] There is no fear if you have no fear. There is nothing to fear. I mean, [I think] you should be a little careful. And they tell us now apparently the early '90s was very bad in New York? I've never noticed the difference; it's always been the same to me. Watch out! Certainly don't go to the Park.

Looking across the span of your films, one could say you've traced the entire arc of the Italian-American experience in New York, starting with Little Italy, the ancestral urban home, but then moving out to the semi-suburban communities of Queens and Brooklyn in Goodfellas *(1990), and finally to the suburbs themselves by the end of that film. One can sense even as early as* Mean Streets, *made in 1973, that the primacy of Little Italy was already threatened by this outward shift, as well as the powerful assimilating forces of New York generally. Did you feel that at the time?*

Totally, totally. Those shots we did in the San Gennaro festival—by that point, the San Gennaro festival was *the* festival; the ones I really wanted to shoot were the San Gandolfo and San Ciro festivals, they were much smaller and they're Sicilian, they were on Elizabeth Street—but by that point they were being phased out. The San Gennaro festival was more commercial, more like a circus, and that was all I could get. It was very different. If I had gotten the Sicilian one, it would have meant a little more to me. But that's all right.

But you carry the story on with Goodfellas, *much of which was set in those distinctive outerborough settings…*

It was a little alien to me, it was outerborough, a little too far "uptown" [*laughs*]…That was pretty much of a stretch for me, quite honestly.

That's also part of New York City…

That *is* part of New York City. And what happened, I felt somewhat at home, because the first few years of my life were spent in Corona, Queens. I was born in Flushing Hospital [in 1942]. At that time, my mother's side of the family, she was one of eight, my father was one of seven or eight, and the thing to do, having grown up with fourteen people in two-and-a-half rooms, was to move out—*not* get an apartment down the block—so Sunnyside, Queens, I think they moved to. And then they found the ground-floor apartment of a two-family house in Corona, Queens, where my mother's mother had moved to, and a number of people on my mother's side of the family. Still there were some on Prince Street. The Scorseses, my father's parents, really stayed in 241 Elizabeth Street. And there was still always the connection with the old neighborhood, people would come back to work, would come back on the weekends, they would shop in the neighborhood. But those leafy streets [in Corona] I remember from the early days, and I remember being very sickly because of my asthma, I remembered there was a tree in the background—I liked that—and then my father got into trouble with the landlord and we had to move back to Elizabeth Street in 1949. And when I looked out the window from my grandmother's at 241, I looked in the street and there were kids running up and down the streets, it was like something out of *Somebody Up There Likes Me*—literally—and I was this sickly kid, and that's what they put me into…

I suppose that was your first New York "location shot" right there, framed by the window…

Yes, right there…*everything* going on in the street: cars, people, butcher shops, groceries, juke boxes, and kids running up and down with garbage pails, playing with them, throwing them at each other, people chasing them with sticks—I mean it was such life, I mean, the meat being delivered, the meat being cut up, the pork store, the fish store on Prince Street, all of this *alive*, you know—and noise, noise to the point of, you can't imagine—all night, with the trucks, 'cause the streets were so small. But in any event, in a funny way those few years in Corona were a comfort to me, so I touched upon those images in *Goodfellas*, you could see it in the club that Paulie [Paul Sorvino] owns, you could see outside the windows those trees, those pathetic trees, with their pathetic leaves, I don't know what they're called….

London plane trees…perhaps the ugliest tree in the world….

The ugliest tree in the world! But it was okay, they're *kind* of green… it was nice and so that's what we touched upon there. As far as living in New Jersey or by the end, Nassau—the Five Towns—I had no idea, I just took the mentality and put it in…

Speaking more generally for a minute, when you are looking at a potential New York location—a side street, for example—for a scene in one of your films, what exactly are you looking for?

I think, first of all, what tells the story of the scene. But for me, the story is told within a certain context, usually a visual one. With the wide frame that we're using—whether it's a 2.35:1 or 1.85:1 aspect ratio—what would that street look like in perspective? How do you get the best out of that street? And only then, can I place the characters in there? And do I show more of the middle of the buildings and the top, or do I show the sidewalk and street, and cut the tops of the buildings off? Because you're always going to be dealing with the widescreen. Or do you just track along the side of the street and have the characters walk? For example in *Raging Bull*, Salvy is talking to Joey—it's Frank Vincent and Joe Pesci—in the beginning of the film, walking in the street before Joey goes up to see his brother, Salvy's saying, why don't your brother play ball with us, and the two of them are walking in a neighborhood street. And we shot it I think up in Hell's Kitchen, and basically it was shot horizontally, so to speak—not down the street, but against the side of the

street, and tracked with Joe and Frank, past [period] cars that were parked there, maybe four or five, that's all, and beyond them were a few people sitting on the stoops, in costume, maybe two or three, maybe one person walking by, and the most [you could see] of the buildings they walked by was the first floor, that's it. And it gives the impression of New York, 1941. And it's nothing, we didn't do anything, we got buildings that happened to be there and put some cars in front!

As someone who has made films on the streets of New York for more than forty years now, how would you describe how the experience has changed over the decades, from the days of Taxi Driver *in 1975, say, to more recent films like* Bringing Out the Dead *(1999) and* The Departed *(2006)?*

Back on *Taxi Driver*, it was a lower budget film, it was more contained, we had a smaller crew than what I have now, than what I had on *The Departed* and *Bringing Out the Dead.* And in a funny way we seemed to fit in better with the city, we became part of the street. There was some rejection, there was some anger, 13th Street between Second and Third Avenue, it was pretty bad, bottles would sometimes come flying at us, but we were still part of the street. We were shooting in the Garment District at one point—I always tell this story—and I took my eye away from the eyepiece, and when I turned back, I couldn't find the camera. There were so many people—and they couldn't care less! My father was coming home from work, with his lunch bag, because he worked in the Garment District, and he said what are you doing? I said we're shooting the film. He couldn't even see the crew. Then a thunderstorm hit. I mean, we were part of the life of the city. Nowadays, that all stops. When I go into a situation now when I'm using big movie stars, and the budget is a certain amount, you're bringing in a small city to another city. It's no longer a few trailers. Now streets are blocked off, lights are set up, with bigger movie stars people come up to them, they have bigger trailers, then they also have a make-up trailer. Some even have a workout trailer. And then if you add two or three stars together, my biggest problem now is that if you want to improvise and move a location right away, it's very difficult, very difficult. But you still learn how to work within that system too.

I think what's happened is that, in a way, the equipment has gone back to the old studio days, only in the streets. The images are beautiful. The cinematography is great. And in a funny way, the city has now become a studio, and so that finally, it's like the people are part of the studio, and they're all movie savvy, too. There's no strange thing about it any more. It's all part of one thing. Everybody's photographing. Everybody's making films. And the city has become the great studio.

MARTY
THE LOST WEEKEND
FORCE OF EVIL
THE NAKED CITY
ON THE TOWN
THE SEVEN YEAR ITCH
ON THE WATERFRONT
12 ANGRY MEN
THE WRONG MAN
NORTH BY NORTHWEST
SWEET SMELL OF SUCCESS
KILLER'S KISS
SHADOWS
LITTLE FUGITIVE
WEST SIDE STORY
BREAKFAST AT TIFFANY'S
A THOUSAND CLOWNS
THE PAWNBROKER
MIRAGE

On street corners, in alleys, avenues, squares and modest flats, screenland's magic boxes are grinding out the color and life of New York for some dozen realistic films. Our townfolk are happy about it. From location to location the tumbling crowds follow, gaping and wondering and primping…

Douglas Gilbert, *New York World-Telegram*, July 21, 1947

JOHN ALTON, CINEMATOGRAPHER, 1949 In exteriors as well as interiors, [prewar] Hollywood was addicted to the candied type of…sweet unreal photography. Then came the war. The enemy was real and could not be present at production meetings. There were no rehearsals on battlefields or during naval or air battles. There was only *one take* for each scene. There were no boosters, no sun reflectors, no butterflies, and no diffusers. The pictures were starkly real. Explosions rocked the cameras, but they also rocked the world, and with it rocked Hollywood out of its old-fashioned ideas about photography. The year 1947 brought a new photographic technique…accepted by the great majority. Let us have more realism.

BEFORE THE MAYOR'S OFFICE

Filming THE LOST WEEKEND (1945) Hollywood had abandoned location shooting in New York for nearly a decade and a half when, in the closing years of World War II, a handful of feature filmmakers began the first tentative forays back onto the streets of the city. The very first was the director Billy Wilder's film version of Charles R. Jackson's groundbreaking fictional portrait of alcoholism. Wilder chose to dramatize an alcoholic's sheer craving for liquor through an unforgettable scene in which his main character, a writer played by Ray Milland, trudges up Third Avenue from 55th to 110th Street, desperate to pawn his typewriter for drink money— and unaware that it is Yom Kippur, the Jewish holiday, for which every pawnshop has been closed. Filming the harrowing sequence across a single Sunday—New Year's Day, 1944, when most of the avenue's shops were indeed shuttered—Wilder hid his cameramen inside bakery trucks and atop store marquees (above) to capture the real life of the street as the exhausted and disheveled Milland, typewriter in hand, wandered the avenue for nearly three miles beneath the roar of its elevated train.

I just kept going down and down there. It was like going down to the bottom of the world.

John Garfield (as Joe Morse) in *Force of Evil*

FORCE OF EVIL (1948) For his screen adaptation of Ira Wolfert's novel, *Tucker's People*, the politically minded filmmaker Abraham Polonsky shot several key sequences on location around Manhattan, tracing in urban terms the moral and psychological descent of his main character, Joe Morse (John Garfield)— a self-made, smooth-talking lawyer who is helping his client, a powerful gangster named Tucker, gain control of the city's numbers racket. As the story comes to a climax Morse realizes his corrupt "big-business" tactics have cost the life of his own brother—a small-time bookie played by Thomas Gomez— and as the film ends Morse makes his final nightmarish descent (above), racing down a stone-faced escarpment near the George Washington Bridge to find his brother's body washed up on the rocky shoreline beneath the girders of the bridge itself. Though some hoped Polonsky's pioneering efforts would give rise to a postwar renaissance of the New York film industry, his career was derailed just a year later by the Hollywood blacklist, and he would not direct another film until *Madigan*, a New York police thriller made in 1968.

This is the city as it is: hot summer pavements, the children at play, the buildings in their naked stone, the people without make-up.

Mark Hellinger (as narrator) in *The Naked City*

THE NAKED CITY (1948)

Based on the original idea of a young screenwriter named Malvin Wald—who had spent his war years making documentary training films for the Air Force—*The Naked City* represented a breakthrough for the American film industry: a talking picture shot almost entirely on location in New York. Produced by the noted columnist Mark Hellinger and directed by Jules Dassin, the film traced the efforts of the city's Homicide Division to locate the murderer of a young woman–an early version of the "police procedural" that would live on in countless later television shows, from the series called "Naked City" (and drawn from the film) to "Law & Order" (see pages 258 and 259). No less innovative was its filmmakers' almost complete reliance on location shooting, working over the summer of 1947 in 107 different locations around the city, including police precincts, East River piers, apartments on Park Avenue and the Upper West Side, fashion boutiques, high-rise construction sites, Toots Shor's restaurant, the city morgue at Bellevue, and streets and neighborhoods from Brooklyn Heights and Astoria, Queens, to Fifth Avenue and the Lower East Side—where a final chase sequence comes to a climax on the walkways and towers of the Williamsburg Bridge (OPPOSITE PAGE AND ABOVE). Though the film proved a major artistic and commercial success, the logistics of location shooting turned out to be more difficult than anticipated—as police failed to control unruly crowds, officials held up shooting in expectation of payoffs, and a host of accidents and incidents plagued the production, pushing the film a half million dollars over budget. *Naked City* would nevertheless demonstrate the unmatched power of the city as a motion picture location, a lesson not lost on a younger generation, including a young photographer assigned by *Look* magazine to cover the production: Stanley Kubrick (seen at right in a suit with his cameras).

CINE-GRAMS, JANUARY 1948 The story…centers on the New York Police Department and its success in tracking down a murderer from scanty clues. Everything else is the city itself—twenty billion dollars' worth of "sets" no studio could reproduce, and more of New York than a visitor would see in a week's touring.

There was no stage, no theatre, simply the street.

Stanley Donen, co-director, *On the Town*

GENE KELLY, CO-DIRECTOR AND ACTOR, *ON THE TOWN* It was only in *On the Town* that we tried something entirely new in the musical film. Live people get off a real ship in the Brooklyn Navy Yard and dance down New York City. We did a lot of quick cutting— we'd be on top of Radio City and then on the bottom—we'd cut from Mulberry Street to Third Avenue—and so the dissolve went out of style. This was one of the things that changed the history of musicals more than anything.

ON THE TOWN (1949) Just a few months after the release of *The Naked City*, another team sought to extend the experiment in location shooting to a new genre. Eager to preserve the fresh spirit and energy of the 1945 Broadway hit musical by Betty Comden, Adolph Green, and Leonard Bernstein—which followed the adventures of three sailors with just one day's leave in New York—the co-directors Stanley Donen and Gene Kelly wanted to shoot the entire film in the city, but in the end were able to obtain permission from MGM to film only the ten-minute opening "New York, New York" sequence on location. The shoot, in May 1949, nevertheless took the cast and crew—including actors Frank Sinatra and Jules Munshin as well as co-directors Kelly and Donen—to dozens of locations around the city, including the Upper Bay (ABOVE), the streets of Little Italy (OPPOSITE, TOP), where a few local residents leaned out of their windows to watch the shooting in progress, and the skating rink at Rockefeller Center (OPPOSITE, BOTTOM), where several hundred New Yorkers did the same, gathering around the edge of the space to watch the trio perform.

Oh, do you feel the breeze from the subway? Isn't it delicious?

Marilyn Monroe (as The Girl)
in *The Seven Year Itch*

NEW YORK JOURNAL-AMERICAN, SEPTEMBER 13, 1954 There won't be any admission charge when Marilyn appears for the shooting of street sequences for the new film, *The Seven Year Itch*. Miss Monroe's costume is expected to be more revealing than the one she wore yesterday to stop the traffic.

Filming THE SEVEN YEAR ITCH (1955) By the early 1950s, Hollywood production crews, though still not common, could be found more frequently filming location sequences in New York for features otherwise produced entirely in Los Angeles. Although these shoots almost invariably attracted the attention of the city's press and passersby, none drew a fraction of the attention—or entered as deeply into the

American imagination—as the scene filmed on location on the chilly night of September 15th, 1954, along Lexington Avenue between 51st and 52nd Streets, for a feature called *The Seven Year Itch*. Under Billy Wilder's direction, the sequence called for Tom Ewell and Marilyn Monroe— then at the peak of her fame— to linger outside the Trans-Lux Theatre as a gust of wind from a passing subway train (actually generated by a large

fan beneath the grating) blew Monroe's dress up around her waist, revealing a glimpse of underwear. Advance notice of the shoot, which began at one a.m., brought out dozens of newspaper photographers and about 1,500 raucous onlookers (a number later exaggerated to five thousand or more), who watched for three hours as a nervous Monroe continually missed her lines, forcing Wilder to call for take after take. The

sidewalk spectacle was later said to have marked an end to Monroe's marriage to Joe DiMaggio, who watched the overt display from the sidelines with growing anger and disgust. In the end, ironically, the footage went unused, as the film's producers decided to reshoot the entire scene on a Fox stage because of supposed problems with the sound quality (some later claimed the New York shoot was actually carried out solely

for publicity purposes, and was never intended for use in the film itself). In the years to come, the stills of Monroe on the sidewalks of New York, her white summer dress billowing, became not only the primary publicity image for the film itself, but one of the most iconic images of modern American popular culture.

OPPOSITE PAGE **Filming ON THE WATERFRONT (1954)** Even as Hollywood studios continued to import location crews to the city in the 1950s, a handful of daring pioneers were exploring a radical alternative: an indigenous New York film industry, turning out features that were not only photographed but produced in the city. It began when the celebrated director Elia Kazan (in dark sweater) and the screenwriter Budd Schulberg chose to film Schulberg's controversial script—an exposé of corruption in the Port of New York—in and around New York itself, including locations shot in Hoboken, New Jersey, just across the Hudson from Manhattan, and stage scenes shot in the ancient Fox Studios on West 55th Street. Turning their back on Hollywood, they tapped the ranks of New York's theater—including the rising star of the Broadway stage, Marlon Brando (in checkered jacket)—and assembled a crew of local craftsmen and technicians, including the cinematographer Boris Kaufman. The success of the film—which won the Academy Award for Best Picture and ten others besides—soon inspired successors such as **MARTY (1955)** (LEFT, TOP), a touching filmic portrait of a Bronx butcher's search for love, adapted from a television drama by Paddy Chayefsky—which itself went on to win the Oscar for Best Picture in 1955.This publicity still, shot in a Bronx store that served as one of the film's interiors, shows the producer Harold Hecht, the director Delbert Mann, the cinematographer Joseph LaShelle, the art director Edward S. Haworth, and the stars Betsy Blair and Ernest Borgnine. LEFT BOTTOM **Filming 12 ANGRY MEN (1957)** In many ways, the real birth of the modern film industry in New York can be traced to *12 Angry Men*, the first feature directed by the man who, more than anyone else, sustained feature film-making in New York before the founding of the Mayor's Office in 1966: Sidney Lumet. A former television director and child actor, Lumet (shown here in white shirt, directing Henry Fonda) shot Reginald Rose's single-room jury drama in an astonishing thirteen weeks, including a brief location scene on the steps of the New York County Courthouse on Foley Square.

ELIA KAZAN Our first day's work was on the rooftops from which the camera could look down the slope of the city of Hoboken to the Hudson River and across the other side, New York City. It was a misty day, and the New York skyline in the distance was visible but gray, frosty and indistinct. I was very disappointed. But what appeared to be our misfortune that morning was a truer value; our view of the famous New York skyline throughout the movie was always gray and indistinct—the opposite of a picture postcard. This created the correct mood for the film, and I wasn't smart enough to realize it immediately. But in time I did, and as I suppose by the old rule that luck evens out, every time we turned our camera east, the sky was gray and threatening and the way I wanted it to be.

Working conditions were murderous. We shot film every day, regardless of the weather. We worked through November and December rain, January and February snow, sleet, slush, and smog. We shot in freezing damp warehouses; on ice-caked piers, in back streets and alleys, tenement rooftops and flats, in churches and parks.

Elia Kazan, director, *On the Waterfront*

LEFT THE WRONG MAN (1956) Though Alfred Hitchcock had already used New York as the setting for several memorable features—*Saboteur, Rope, Rear Window*—he had always followed conventional studio practice and recreated the city on the Hollywood lot. For *The Wrong Man*, a film based on the true story of a musician accused of a string of hold-ups in Queens, the director decided to shoot the picture entirely on location—and, to the greatest degree possible, in the exact locations where the actual events had occurred. Yet for all the careful precision of its settings— and its striking, documentary-like glimpses of mid-1950s midtown and Jackson Heights, Queens—the film offers a deeply expressionistic portrait of an ordinary New York man and his family being engulfed in a nightmarish situation. In this scene, near the start of the film, Manny Balestrero (Henry Fonda) heads home late at night from his job at the Stork Club, descending into the subway at 53rd Street and Fifth Avenue under the eyes of a watchful yet somehow sinister-seeming policeman.

JAY COCKS, SCREENWRITER *The Wrong Man* was shot entirely on location. And what you've got is the documentary locations, the real locations, which become very literal, and these extremely subjective, figurative camera moves. This extraordinary staging… makes it seem as if this city we live in has all of a sudden become a dreamscape, but a dreamscape for a nightmare, and the kind of nightmare that could happen to any one of us.

LEFT Filming **NORTH BY NORTHWEST** (1959) Gradually embracing the use of locations as the 1950s progressed, Hitchcock shot several major scenes for *North By Northwest* in various spots around Manhattan, including a Madison Avenue sidewalk, the lobbies of the Plaza Hotel, and the interior of Grand Central Terminal—where a New York businessman named Roger Thornhill (Cary Grant), wanted for a murder he didn't commit, relies on the rushing crowds of the Main Concourse to stay unnoticed as he tries to board the Twentieth Century Limited for Chicago.

ROBERT BOYLE, PRODUCTION DESIGNER, *NORTH BY NORTHWEST* Hitchcock…has never felt comfortable with real locations, perhaps because he can't control them as finely. On *North by Northwest* we actually used Grand Central Station rather than reconstructing it on the set. The amount of light we poured into that station almost broke MGM.

SWEET SMELL OF SUCCESS (1957) Based on a scorching screenplay by Clifford Odets and Ernest Lehman—a fictionalized exposé of the all-powerful New York columnist, Walter Winchell—the film was directed by the Englishman Alexander Mackenrick and photographed by the legendary Hollywood camera-man James Wong Howe, who took advantage of recent advances in camera lenses and film stock to shoot much of the picture on location in New York by night. In this scene, among the last in the film and one of the few to take place in daylight, a press agent named Sidney Falco (Tony Curtis) approaches Susan Hunsecker (Susan Harrison)—the sister of the columnist J.J. Hunsecker (the Winchell-like figure, played by Burt Lancaster)—who has at last decided to leave her brother and the seamy nocturnal world he represents.

I love this dirty town.
Burt Lancaster (as J.J. Hunsecker) in *Sweet Smell of Success*

KILLER'S KISS (1957)
Throughout the 1950s, deter-mined filmmakers sought to sidestep the traditional studio system by producing feature films on their own. Shooting without any city permits and using borrowed equipment (such as a springwound Ey-emo camera, which held a 100-foot film magazine) the 27 year-old photographer

Stanley Kubrick filmed his first feature length film in locations across the city, from Times Square and Pennsylvania Station to the antenna-filled rooftops of lower Manhattan, where Frank Silvera—playing a corrupt nightclub boss—attempts to outrun the film's lead, a prizefighter played by Jamie Smith.

SHADOWS (1959) Described by Leonard Maltin as "a water-shed in the birth of American independent cinema," Cassa-vetes' first feature—a loosely structured, semi-improvised story about a young, light-skinned black woman (Lelia Goldoni) and her brothers—was filmed with a handheld 16mm camera on locations that ranged from apartments

and jazz clubs to 42nd Street, Central Park, and the Museum of Modern Art. The power and immediacy of the resulting film—and the fact that it had been produced without studio financing or distribution—helped to galvanize an entire generation of aspiring New York filmmakers, including a young NYU student named Martin Scorsese (see page 24).

Actor John Cassavetes can be seen roaming the Broadway area these nights, trailing a camera and an entourage of young actors, writers, friends and cautious policemen.

New York World-Telegram and the Sun, February 10th, 1957

JOHN CASSAVETES, DIRECTOR, *SHADOWS* I gave [the actors] neighborhoods to go to and then we would shoot in those neighborhoods. They hung around Broadway and different places downtown…And then when we finally started shooting, they had assimilated. They pretty much became the people they were playing.

LITTLE FUGITIVE (1953) Years before Kubrick or Cassavetes, a trio of young photographers—Morris Engel, his wife Ruth Orkin, and friend named Raymond Abrashkin (working under the pseudonym "Ray Ashley") decided to make a feature-length, 35mm film by themselves. Working with an inventor he had known in the Navy, Engel developed a handheld camera rig—an ancestor of the modern day Steadicam (see page 226)—that allowed he and his colleagues to move about almost unnoticed through the public spaces of Coney Island to shoot their film, the story of a young Brooklyn boy (Richie Andrusco) who spends a forbidden weekend sampling the fabled amusement park's attractions before being hauled home by his brother. Like Cassavetes' efforts, the lasting impact of Engel and his partners lay not only in their film's spontaneous and authentic feel, but in their daring decision to avoid the compromises of the studio. "Our New Wave would never have come into being," the French director François Truffaut later acknowledged, "if it hadn't been for Morris Engel, who showed us the way to independent production with *Little Fugitive*."

I had the strange idea that a couple of people with the right equipment could compete with Hollywood for next to no money. It was a heretical concept.

Morris Engel, co-director, *Little Fugitive*

ROBERT WISE, CO-DIRECTOR, *WEST SIDE STORY* I felt we needed to open the film in its milieu, in the real streets, alleys and playgrounds of New York. One key location was where Lincoln Center is now. The block was going to be torn down to make way for the Center, and we got there just before the contractor started tearing it own. On one shot in which George Chakiris and three of the Sharks do some dance steps in the foreground, we went very low with the camera and got this big striking background of tenements with their marvelous color and great style.

ARTHUR KNIGHT, *SATURDAY REVIEW*, OCTOBER 1961 On a bitingly cold February morning in 1960, I found myself in a huge vacant lot in Manhattan's West Sixties. Everywhere, groups of shivering figures were huddled about trash can fires, stamping their feet on the frozen ground and the loose rubble. Beyond them stood half a block of boarded tenements destined for demolition....Out on a rise, surveying the debris of a ruined city, stood a single camera, its crew blowing on their hands and muttering in articulate puffs of vapor. Then suddenly, over the rise, dashed four youngsters in summer shirts, blue jeans, and sneakers, their leaps and outflung arms filled with the joy of living. It was the start of filming on *West Side Story*.

WEST SIDE STORY (1961)

Charged with bringing the groundbreaking Broadway musical to the screen, the co-directors Robert Wise and Jerome Robbins (who also functioned as choreographer) sought to shoot as much of the film as possible on the actual streets of the city, but as in *On the Town*, a decade earlier, the location sequences were ultimately reserved for a single extended musical scene that opens the film. Working primarily on West 68th Street, on tenement blocks that were already being razed to make way for Lincoln Center (note the empty and boarded windows in the background), the film dramatized the city's growing racial tensions by presenting a power struggle between two street gangs—the native-born "Jets" (ABOVE) and the Puerto Rican "Sharks," (OPPOSITE, TOP) —largely in balletic terms, using a dance style devised by Robbins (OPPOSITE, BOTTOM) that became, in Gerald Mast's words, "an unforgettable image of reaching for the sky and longing for space." Though camera tests began on a bitterly cold day in February 1960, with snow still on the ground, actual shooting did not proceed until August that year, in some of the hottest weather on record. LEFT Before the cameras rolled each morning, on-lookers were intrigued and amused to see the supposedly violent teenage "gangs" engaged in classical ballet stretches and exercises, using a tenement fence as a makeshift barre.

JEROME ROBBINS, CO-DIRECTOR, *WEST SIDE STORY* The four or five blocks had all been condemned and we got there just before they started. There was this one ideal street, and we managed to get to the contractor and give him a little money under the table and have him start on one of the other streets, and let us have them. But we didn't have a playground. We found an ideal playground on East 110th Street, straight in the heart of the Puerto Rican area. So what you see in the opening is a combination of West Side and East Side. The dancers would jump up on the West Side and come down on the East Side.

It was the first time the venerable establishment had been invaded by the cinema, and, opined one incredulous executive, it would almost certainly be the last.

Life Magazine, September 1961

**BREAKFAST AT TIFFANY'S
(1961) Among the most endur-
ingly romantic of all sequences
filmed in New York in the years
before the Mayor's Office
are those in Blake Edwards'
screen adaptation of Tru-
man Capote's 1958 novella,
"Breakfast at Tiffany's."
Though most of the film's
interiors were constructed** on a Paramount sound stage,
Edwards chose to shoot
several key exterior scenes
on location, most notably
the film's opening sequence,
set just after dawn, showing Audrey Hepburn as Holly
Golightly—still wearing a
Givenchy evening dress from
the night before—staring
dreamily into a gem-filled Tiffany's window as she
consumes a "breakfast" of
take-out coffee and a Danish
(ABOVE). Aware that Hepburn
disliked performing in front of
strangers, Edwards sought to
avoid onlookers by working
very early on a Sunday morning, but the presence of police
units at the corner of Fifth
Avenue and 57th Street made passersby assume a jewel
heist was in progress, and
a crowd gathered anyway.
Later that day, Edwards took
his cast and crew inside the
main selling floor of the store,
which had hired twenty extra
guards to protect its twenty-
five million dollars' worth of
merchandise. Other location
sequences in the film included several shots outside the East
71st Street row house of Holly
and her neighbor Paul Varjak
(George Peppard) (OPPOSITE
PAGE, TOP), and an extended
pursuit that concludes at
the Naumburg Bandshell in
Central Park, where Varjak
confronts a mysterious
stranger played by Buddy
Ebsen (OPPOSITE BOTTOM).

THE PAWNBROKER (1965)

A common source for New York location films in the mid-1960s were novels whose dark themes and characters made them inappropriate for glossy Hollywood productions. Edward Lewis Wallant's 1961 novel—about an aging Holocaust survivor eking out his days as an uncaring pawnbroker in East Harlem—was transformed by the director

Sidney Lumet in 1965 into a classic New York movie. The film was shot substantially in and around a weathered pawnshop run by Sol Nazerman (Rod Steiger)—a set constructed by the art director Boris Kaufman using the exterior and interior of an empty storefront on Park Avenue and 116th Street. (This desire for continuity between inside and out—almost unheard-of

in feature film production— would also drive the approach to *Dog Day Afternoon*, as described on page 63). This eerily realistic image, showing police rushing to aid a shooting victim while attempting to hold off onlookers, was taken during the film's climax, after Nazerman's Puerto Rican assistant (Jesus Ortiz) is shot while trying to protect his boss.

SIDNEY LUMET, DIRECTOR, *THE PAWNBROKER* For that scene, we had three hidden cameras outside the shop. When the shots were fired, neighborhood people were walking by. They were unaware a movie was being made. We just decided to fire the gun and let it happen. Whether it's through my own knowledge of the city or something else I can't explain. I had the confidence to know something extraordinary would happen—and it did.

Filming A THOUSAND CLOWNS (1965) By the mid-1960s, a handful of producers and directors (usually with financing and distribution deals from United Artists, the traditional maverick among Hollywood studios) were attempting to transform successful Broadway plays into films shot in New York, in the hope that filming on real locations would "open up" stage-bound scripts while preserving their urban texture and authenticity. The screen version of Herb Gardner's hit 1962 play, adapted by Gardner himself, was filmed in its entirety in the city by Fred Coe, a former television director and producer fully aware of the limits of New York's then-nascent production facilities. As a consequence, much of the film was shot outdoors, in locations ranging from Central Park and Fifth Avenue to the Upper West Side and Wall Street. Many of the film's most visually striking sequences were filmed around New York Bay, where the unemployed TV writer Murray Burns (Jason Robards, seen here on Ellis Island with Barry Gordon who plays his nephew) chooses to remove himself from the bustle and fray of the commercial city.

LEFT MIRAGE (1965) Directed by Edward Dmytryk and based on the novel *Fallen Angel* by Howard Fast (under the pseudonym Walter Ericson), this psychological thriller featured Gregory Peck as a mid-level New York businessman named David Stillwell, who attempts to reconstruct his missing past while escaping a group of professional gunmen out to kill him. His journey takes him across the city, from the office towers of lower Manhattan to the promenade at Battery Park to the bucolic landscape of Central Park—from which he barely escapes with his life. Along the way, the city not only offers a series of clues to his dilemma but, through its very size and anonymity, helps keep him alive. Produced the year before the founding of the Mayor's Office, *Mirage* was one of only two films that year to be shot in its entirety in the city (the other was *A Thousand Clowns*)—and one of only thirteen features to include any location shooting in New York at all.

THE PRODUCERS
ROSEMARY'S BABY
MIDNIGHT COWBOY
KLUTE
SERPICO
THE TAKING OF PELHAM ONE TWO THREE
THE FRENCH CONNECTION
THREE DAYS OF THE CONDOR
DOG DAY AFTERNOON
COOGAN'S BLUFF
DEATH WISH
YOU'RE A BIG BOY NOW
NO WAY TO TREAT A LADY
THE APRIL FOOLS
COTTON COMES TO HARLEM
GREETINGS
GODSPELL
UP THE DOWN STAIRCASE
BAREFOOT IN THE PARK
THE PANIC IN NEEDLE PARK
NEXT STOP, GREENWICH VILLAGE
SHAFT
THE PRISONER OF SECOND AVENUE
REPORT TO THE COMMISSIONER
THE WIZ
KING KONG
WOLFEN

The history of art
is the history
of great cities.
There is a hysteria
about New York,
its very ugliness
makes it beautiful.
It has the highest
energy level of
any city in the world.
When you shoot here,
it's like sitting on a
big lid ready to blow
sky high. And this
energy reaches
the screen.
Sidney Lumet, director, 1967

VINCENT CANBY, *NEW YORK TIMES*, 1974 When filmmakers arrived to work here in quantity, they began to make movies that weren't simply set in New York but were also about New York. The image of New York in contemporary movies has as much to do with changes in the American film industry over the last 20 years as it has to do with the continuing collapse of New York. It has to do with the decline of the Hollywood studios—physically and psychologically— with the conviction of an increasing number of filmmakers that movies should be made on location as often as possible (one result of the influence of foreign films of the fifties), and with the emergence of what might be called the regional or environmental American film, the film in which the locale may be as important as the plot.

EARLY YEARS OF THE MAYOR'S OFFICE

It irritated me that the New York film scene was languishing. We had the talent, a vast variety of skills and locations, everything a filmmaker would want for shooting in a big city.

Mayor John V. Lindsay, May 1967

In the first few years after the founding of the Mayor's Office of Film, Theatre, and Broadcasting, Mayor John V. Lindsay made a habit of visiting nearly every film being shot substantially on location in the city, officially to demonstrate the depth of his commitment to encouraging local production; unofficially, to share in some of the glamour and excitement of the burgeoning local film industry. His rounds included a visit to the location setting in East Harlem of UP THE DOWN STAIRCASE (1967) (RIGHT), where he sat for publicity stills with the film's cast and producers, including the actress Sandy Dennis (standing behind the Mayor, pointing), and the author Bel Kaufman (sitting beside the Mayor), who had written the bestselling novel upon which the film was based. Noted himself for enjoying "mati-nee-idol looks," the Mayor felt at home with figures from the entertainment world and on more than one occasion dropped his formal demeanor to cavort around the set with actors and crew. On the morning of August 29, 1966— just twelve weeks after issuing the executive order that led to the founding of the Mayor's Office of Film, Theatre and Broadcasting— Mayor Lindsay paid a visit to a location for LUV (1967), one of the first productions to take advantage of the city's new, streamlined permit process. Press photographers caught this image of Lindsay playing out a frivolous version of the scene in progress, in which a suicidal character, played by Jack Lemmon, is dissuaded by a stranger (Peter Falk) from jumping over the rail of the Manhattan Bridge. (OPPOSITE).

NEWSWEEK, MAY 29, 1967 "Only a year ago," recalls one New York City official, "people in Hollywood felt nobody in his right mind would film in New York unless he absolutely had to—and if he had to, that he'd better get in and out as fast as hell." But that was a year ago, before Mayor John V. Lindsay launched his vigorous campaign to restore New York to the filmmaking capital it was during the early days of motion pictures. Last week, the traffic in Manhattan was as deadly as ever, the weather as uncertain, but the city itself had suddenly become a movie set teeming with armies of extras, crews and crowds. New York was back in the film business full-time.

DAVID SUSSKIND, PRODUCER, 1967 It's absolutely amazing—what the Mayor has done, I mean. Used to be that we had red tape running out of our ears, what with getting permits for every location that was used. If, for instance, you wanted to shoot a TV segment, or a film, using 17 different locations in the city, you had to have 17 different permits. The paperwork was monstrous and you had the police in every precinct where you were shooting checking you out to see if you had violated any laws and…well now you get one permit and it covers any and every location you want to use… anywhere in the city!

1966–1975

The Lincoln Center scene was the great thrill of my life. That was the last day of filming. We got there just as the sun was going to set, and when the water shot up behind me and as I was running around [the fountain] I said, "I'd like to do this for the rest of my life." It was a great scene, and we didn't finish until just about when the sun broke through, and we all went to breakfast at the Brasserie, and had bacon and eggs.

Gene Wilder, actor, *The Producers*

OPPOSITE **THE PRODUCERS (1968)** "I'll *do* it!" the timid New York accountant Leo Bloom (Gene Wilder) shouts out loud, after succumbing to the tempting visions ("wine, women, and song—and women") of a persuasive Broadway producer—and would-be partner—named Max Bialystock (Zero Mostel). His decision is magically (and spectacularly) confirmed when the Metropolitan Opera suddenly lights up behind them and Lincoln Center's fountain explodes into the night sky. Releasing his inner child, Bloom starts running giddily around the fountain, gulping spoonfuls of ice-cream from Max—who also manages to reserve several spoonfuls for himself.

ABOVE **Filming ROSEMARY'S BABY (1968)** Working for the first time in the United States, the Polish-born director Roman Polanski decided to film much of *Rosemary's Baby* on location in New York, underscoring the film's otherworldly horror by placing it within the commonplace settings of ordinary city life. Here he films the frightened, pregnant Rosemary Woodhouse (Mia Farrow) in a phone booth on Fifth Avenue and 62nd Street. In the background sits the garden and townhouse of Mrs. Marcellus Hartley Dodge, the last private freestanding mansion in New York—until its demolition in 1977 for an apartment house.

Photograph courtesy of Museum of the Moving Image / Munkacsi Collection.

Hey! I'm walking here!

Dustin Hoffman, as "Ratso" Rizzo, in *Midnight Cowboy*

MIDNIGHT COWBOY (1969)
Joe Buck (Jon Voight), a
newcomer from Texas who
has come to New York with
dreams of striking it rich as
a hustler—but who has had
trouble, ever since, in keeping
up with Manhattan's fast-
moving pace—here learns
a trick or two from a newfound acquaintance, a small-
time swindler and street

character named "Ratso"
Rizzo (Dustin Hoffman). Deep
in conversation, Rizzo blithely
walks into traffic at 58th
Street and Sixth Avenue—
then angrily berates the driver
of an oncoming car. (He later
confides to Joe that the same
tactic, carried out a bit further
and on purpose, can be a use-
ful way to pick up extra cash.)

MARTIN BREGMAN, PRODUCER, *SERPICO* There was a time when Al would take his character from the sound stage into the street. I mean it's very hard when you're playing this kind of a character not to continue the character [off the set], and there were times when he would walk through the streets in areas where he shouldn't have been walking, because they were relatively dangerous. But he did. He wanted to get the feel of what Frank [Serpico] was doing. And it translated into the character that he did on the film.

Two location-shot films in the early 1970s, SERPICO (1973) and THE FRENCH CONNECTION (1971), were based closely on the experiences of several real-life New York plainclothesmen. ABOVE Sidney Lumet's camera follows Al Pacino, as the honest but outcast undercover cop Frank Serpico, as he makes his way across a tenement rooftop in Williamsburgh, Brooklyn.

RIGHT On a street in lower Manhattan, *The French Connection's* director, William Friedkin, lays out a scene with Gene Hackman and Roy Scheider, playing Jimmy "Popeye" Doyle and his partner Buddy "Cloudy" Russo—characters modeled on the NYPD narcotics detectives Eddie Egan and Sonny Grosso, who broke the actual "French Connection" drug-smuggling case.

WILLIAM FRIEDKIN We built no sets. Everything is shot on actual locations, very often the locations where the [actual events] occurred.

One of the things we were trying to do is give you a different view of New York. All of the aspects of New York, high and low. Really in many ways I felt this was a kind of crude poem to the city.

William Friedkin, director,
The French Connection

THREE DAYS OF THE CONDOR (1975) After his entire research division is brutally (and mysteriously) assassinated, a bookish CIA analyst played by Robert Redford—stunned, confused, and terrified for his life— tries to contact agency headquarters from the protective anonymity of a public phone booth on Riverside Drive, just north of 124th Street. Reflections in the glass subtly hint at the film's sudden sense of ambiguity, disorientation, and unreality.

New York is a city where one can get a more intense view of our society than any place in the world.

Alan J. Pakula, director, *Klute*

KLUTE (1971) Searching for clues to the disappearance of a missing colleague, a soft-spoken Pennsylvania detective named John Klute (Donald Sutherland)—in unlikely alliance with a cynical, hard-edged New York call girl named Bree Daniels (Jane Fonda)—walks down a shabby tenement block in East Harlem (123rd Street, near First Avenue).

ALAN J. PAKULA New York…functioned for us in many ways. I think if we had shot [the picture] within the confines and protections of the film studio, protected from all of the inconveniences, all of the street pain that you see, and all the discomfort and the agony, the picture might have had less intensity and less immediacy, certainly for all of us concerned in making it.

ABOVE AND OVERLEAF **DOG DAY AFTERNOON (1974) Based on an actual 1972 bank robbery attempt which took place just a few miles away, Sidney Lumet's film was shot almost in its entirety on a quiet stretch of shopfronts on Prospect Park West between 17th and 18th Streets, just south of Park Slope, Brooklyn—a space transformed by the robbery in progress, as well as by the charged antics of Sonny Wortzik (Al Pacino), into an impromptu outdoor theater (see pages 6–7).**

SIDNEY LUMET Because so much of the action took place inside the bank, it would've been simpler to build the bank in the studio. But I felt it would be better for staging and the camera if I could move freely between the bank and the street. We came up with the perfect solution. We found an excellent street that had a [street-level] warehouse floor we could rent. We built the bank inside the warehouse so I could have my "wild walls" and still have constant access between the street and the interior of the bank.

OPPOSITE **THE TAKING OF PELHAM ONE TWO THREE** (1974) **To provide the film's startlingly authentic locations, the producers gained permission to reopen a stretch of actual subway tunnel, outside Court Street station, Brooklyn, that had been closed since 1946. For a payment of $250,000 to the Transit Authority—along with another $75,000 for insurance—the filmmakers rented the station, the track, and several subway cars—along with the services of fifteen transit employees, including motormen and technicians. So close was the film's set to active subway lines that several times an hour, for a few frightening moments, the headlights of nearby A and E trains arriving at the Hoyt-Schermerhorn station seemed to be bearing down on the cast and crew.** RIGHT **The station was used again for the filming of late-night confrontations between the self-appointed urban vigilante Charles Bronson and assorted muggers in the controversial 1975 feature,** DEATH WISH.

NEW YORK LANDMARKS
1966–1975

YOU'RE A BIG BOY NOW (1967) Thanks to the personal intercession of Mayor John V. Lindsay, the director Francis Ford Coppola was permitted to shoot his first feature film within the NEW YORK PUBLIC LIBRARY'S central building on Fifth Avenue—including this scene of Peter Kastner, on roller skates, retrieving books from the sprawling stacks.

ROMAN POLANSKI, DIRECTOR, *ROSEMARY'S BABY* My first request [after deciding to direct *Rosemary's Baby*] was [to work with] the production designer Dick Sylbert. Dick told me, there is a building you must see; it's the Dakota. So when we went to New York that was the first place he showed me. I don't know if Ira Levin had the Dakota in mind when he was writing the novel, but that was our immediate decision.

ROSEMARY'S BABY (1968)

The setting of the fictional "Branford" apartment house of Ira Levin's novel, inspired by the ornate Alwyn Court apartment house on West 58th Street, was shifted for the film to the equally picturesque but notably grimmer DAKOTA, a Romanesque Revival structure at Central Park West and 72nd Street, built in 1885 by the architect Henry J. Hardenbergh as one of the city's earliest and most luxurious apartment houses. (The building's dark reputation, initiated in part by its prominent appearance in *Rosemary's Baby*, was sealed a dozen years later by the murder of John Lennon in the same entrance archway visible in this view.)

GREETINGS (1968) Directed and co-written by Brian de Palma at the height of the Vietnam War, this low-budget feature includes several forays by Robert De Niro and his draft-age friends to the U.S. ARMY INDUCTION CENTER at 39 Whitehall Street in lower Manhattan, a stolid granite structure where, between 1886 and 1972, more than three million Americans made the transition from civilian to military life. (It has since been remodeled into a modern, glass-fronted health club.)

RIGHT YOU'RE A BIG BOY NOW (1966) A fantasy sequence featuring Rosemary Harris offers a last glimpse of the shuttered but still standing STEEPLECHASE PARK IN CONEY ISLAND, just weeks before its final destruction in September 1966. The legendary establishment, opened in 1897, was the first and longest lasting of the area's great amusement parks.

OPPOSITE PAGE THE APRIL FOOLS (1969) Unlike the outright destruction of Steeplechase Park or the obliteration of the Army Induction Center's stone facade, the transformation of the city's landmarks over time can sometimes be a more subtle, yet no less revealing affair. In this view, Jack Lemmon, playing (as he so often did) the typical contemporary businessman, strides across the starkly abstract plaza of the then newly completed Marine Midland Bank building at 140 BROADWAY in lower Manhattan, designed by the architects Skidmore, Owings & Merrill and featuring a 28-foot-tall artwork, *Cube*, by the sculptor Isamu Noguchi. In the years since 9/11, the simple modern elegance of the original composition—along with the sense of optimism and openness that lay behind it—has been quietly but profoundly compromised by the installation of security bollards and other barriers.

GODSPELL

Based on the hit Broadway show by a 22 year-old Carnegie-Mellon student named John-Michael Tebelak, **GODSPELL**— a musical adaptation of the Gospel According to St. Matthew—was filmed over "forty days and forty nights" in the summer of 1973 in what was, at the time, the widest and most original use of New York locations in a single feature. The filmmakers sought to achieve both relevance and timelessness by setting their retelling of the story of Jesus and his apostles within a contemporary urban landscape, hauntingly devoid of any people or activity. Inaugurated with a prayer service by a minister from the Cathedral Church of St. John the Divine, shooting began in front of the Empire Diner on Tenth Avenue and 22nd Street, then proceeded all across the city: beneath the Triborough Bridge on Randall's Island (OPPOSITE, UPPER LEFT), atop the Bethesda Fountain in Central Park (OPPOSITE, UPPER RIGHT); on the uncompleted roof of the north tower of the World Trade Center (OPPOSITE, LOWER RIGHT); in the Ramble in Central Park (OPPOSITE, LOWER LEFT); on the Accutron watch sign on Times Square (THIS PAGE, ABOVE), on the neoclassical Soldiers' and Sailors' Monument in Riverside Park (THIS PAGE, UPPER RIGHT), and around the fountain and plazas of Lincoln Center (THIS PAGE, MIDDLE RIGHT AND LOWER RIGHT).

GREENWICH VILLAGE AND WASHINGTON SQUARE PARK

BAREFOOT IN THE PARK (1967) For the screen version of Neil Simon's hit Broadway play, the walk-up apartment of newlyweds Corrie and Paul Bratter (Jane Fonda and Robert Redford) was relocated from the East 40s to the more picturesque and Bohemian blocks of Greenwich Village, just west of Washington Square Park—where the straight-laced Paul, exiled from his apartment, spends the night on a bench and, drunken and shoeless, performs a spirited (if some-what sloppy) dance the next morning.

PAUL MAZURSKY We had to recreate all of this [period setting]. Some of the same shops were there, but we had to get rid of all kinds of paraphernalia—the car-parking junk, television aerials—put up different signs, dress the extras.

The main center for Bohemia at that time was Greenwich Village…the Village was the place. [Many of] the people who lived in the Village [at that time] became famous: Allen Ginsberg, Kerouac, and Dylan Thomas—who I would see at the White Horse, a bar in the West Village.

Paul Mazursky, writer/director, *Next Stop, Greenwich Village*

NEXT STOP, GREENWICH VILLAGE (1975) Paul Mazursky's semi-autobiographical film recreates his years as a young actor in the Village; in this view, Lenny Lapinsky (the director's alter-ego, played by Lenny Baker, last in line) and his friends dance the conga across MacDougal Street, redressed to the film's historical period, 1953. BELOW The basement apartment of Connie (Dory Brenner, far left) and its adjacent stoop on MacDougal Street provide a convenient way-station for Lenny and his circle, which also includes, left to right: Robert (Christopher Walken), Sarah (Ellen Greene), and Bernstein (Antonio Fargas).

CRUISING (1980) For years an insular, late-night enclave of sex clubs and leather bars, the waterfront blocks of the far West Village became the setting in 1980 for William Friedkin's controversial film, starring Al Pacino as an undercover detective who poses as a gay man to solve a string of murders in the area.

ABOVE KIDS (1995) Larry Clark's unsparing portrait of urban adolescence centers on Washington Square Park, which serves as an unsupervised outdoor living room for the film's young cast (including Chloe Sevigny, second from left, joined in this view by the screenwriter Harmony Korinne, just right of center).

ABOVE In SEARCHING FOR BOBBY FISCHER (1993), ten year-old Josh Waitzkin (Max Pomeranc) finds himself gravitating to the legendary cluster of tables at the southeast corner of Washington Square Park, "chess alley," where generations of New Yorkers—including a young Stanley Kubrick in the early 1950s, and, a few years later, Bobby Fischer himself—have come to match their skill against the regulars and hustlers (such as the one portrayed by Lawrence Fishburne, left) who play "blitz chess" for a few dollars a game.

ABOVE WHEN HARRY MET SALLY...(1989) Located in the heart of Washington Square and at the foot of Fifth Avenue, Stanford White's 1895 Washington Arch offers a symbolic "gateway" for two newcomers (played by Billy Crystal and Meg Ryan) who, just as they are greeting the city, believe they are saying farewell to each other.

CHASES

McClane: The fastest way is through the park.

Carver: I told you the park drives are always jammed.

McClane: I didn't say park drives. I said through the *park*.

Bruce Willis and Samuel L. Jackson, in *Die Hard: With a Vengeance*

DIE HARD: WITH A VENGEANCE (1995) Hoping to foil a bombing downtown, policeman John McClane (Bruce Willis) commandeers a taxi and races across the lawns and pathways of Central Park—before leaping over the park's outer wall and directly into the traffic on Central Park South.

15 MINUTES (2001) Detective Eddie Flemming (Robert De Niro) and arson investigator Jordy Warsaw (Ed Burns) race down Madison Avenue in pursuit of two homicide suspects. Shot on a Sunday in July 1999 in 106-degree heat—one of the highest ever recorded in the city—the chase scene required closing the avenue for six blocks, from 60th to 66th Street. (Many of the pedestrians in the background were ordinary New Yorkers, happening on the scene, with no idea a film was being made.) Close-up shots of Burns and De Niro are captured with a lightweight Panaflex camera, stabilized by a handheld Steadicam rig (see page 226) and carried on an all-terrain vehicle.

THE COWBOY WAY (1994)
In the film's spectacular (if slightly outlandish) climax, Kiefer Sutherland and Woody Harrelson, playing New Mexico rodeo riders in New York, take to horseback to chase a murderous smuggler escaping by subway across the Manhattan Bridge.

RIGHT With plywood placed above the subway tracks to overcome the horses' natural aversion to galloping over track ties, the veteran stuntman Troy Gilbert (standing in for Harrelson) makes the leap from horse to subway car, two hundred feet above the East River.

I was very conscious
of the fact that
there had been a great
cop movie made a
couple of years before,
called *Bullitt,* with a
wonderful chase,
two cars on the streets
of San Francisco.
And I didn't want to
do two cars chasing
through the streets
of New York.
So I racked my brains
as to what might be
a little different.
And along with the
producer, Phil D'Antoni,
just walking around
the city, we came up
with the idea of a car
chasing a train.

William Friedkin, director, *The French Connection*

he car-and-subway sequence in HE FRENCH CONNECTION .971)—probably the best-nown chase in New York lms—required five weeks complete, working on and bove a thirty-block stretch f 86th Street in Brooklyn, om the Bay 50th Street ation to the 62nd Street tation of the D line (renamed he N line in the film). A New ork City traffic department ngineer—paid for by 20th entury-Fox—remained on

the set for ten days, changing lights from red to green and back as shooting required. OPPOSITE PAGE At the insistence of the Transit Authority, who refused to allow an actor to sit at the controls, an actual TA motorman played the role of the train operator. The subway car used in the scene, Number 4572, was renovated after the filming and was still running decades later on the M and Z lines. BOTTOM LEFT To capture

behind-the-wheel close-ups of Gene Hackman, the director William Friedkin and the cinematographer Owen Roizman replaced the car's right front seat with a battery-driven Arriflex 2C camera, then tied down the rig with rigid electrical conduit to a plywood board, in order to reduce its movement as the vehicle raced across the pavement.

WILLIAM FRIEDKIN We choreographed the [chase scene]; there were a few stunt cars involved, but not many, and every time there was supposed to be a near-miss with a stunt car, it resulted in a crash. So we had to constantly repair the car that Hackman was in because it was getting beaten up by the stunt cars who were missing their marks. Meanwhile, there were other civilian cars on the streets that had no idea of what we were doing. I had no reservations about doing it then because I was a callow, heedless youth, but I wouldn't do anything like this now.

TOP TO BOTTOM, LEFT TO RIGHT

REPORT TO THE COMMISSIONER (1975)

In what was perhaps the most ambitious chase sequence ever attempted on the streets of New York, a police officer named Bo Lockley (Michael Moriarty) and his partner Richard "Crunch" Blackstone (Yaphet Kotto) chase a suspect named Thomas "Stick" Henderson (Tony King)—clothed only in his underwear—across the heart of midtown Manhattan, from the roof of the Winter Garden Theater on Times Square, down a rod supporting the theater's marquee, onto a passing truck, and across the car roofs of Seventh Avenue's traffic, while dodging a legless indigent veteran (played by Bob Balaban) along the way. The chase continues to Fifth Avenue, where Henderson—with Lockley just steps behind him—races down the sidewalk and into the first floor of Saks Fifth Avenue, past its elegant perfume counters, until reaching a point-blank standoff in an elevator of the venerable department store.

LOWER MANHATTAN AND THE WORLD TRADE CENTER

SIDNEY LUMET, DIRECTOR, *THE WIZ* In the [film's] most expensive sequence, shot at the World Trade Center, we never figured how brutal the wind could be when it was channeled between those two towers. They formed a natural wind tunnel. The hats of the male and female models were important in establishing "attitude." And the hats wouldn't stay on because of the wind. Pins didn't work. Bands around the back of the head wouldn't work. Finally, the bands were placed below the chin. The hats stayed on, but the look was ruined.

THE WIZ (1978) Intended as a witty send-up of New Yorkers' slavish devotion to new trends, the film's most elaborate production number was set on the plaza of the newly completed World Trade Center. The ambitious set, designed by Tony Walton, featured a 24-foot grand piano (played by Quincy Jones), encircled by a translucent Plexiglas dance floor—illuminated from below by 27,000 lamps—that shifted from red to green to gold, as four hundred dancing extras obediently followed commands to discard one colored outfit for another. Shooting the scene—which required four nights and a quarter million dollars to complete—proved a nightmare, as high winds funneling between the towers wrenched loose the floor panels and sent huge sheets of plywood flying thirty and forty stories into the air.

KLUTE (1971) The shadowy character at the heart of Alan Pakula's thriller (Charles Cioffi) occupies an office high up in an ominous, black-skinned skyscraper, through whose stark, floor-to-ceiling windows can be seen rising the even taller and larger towers of the World Trade Center—the very embodiment, for the filmmakers of that time, of the soulless new world coming into being. Seen today, the view of the still uncompleted towers serves instead as a reminder of the extraordinary human effort that went into their construction. At right, the north tower has topped out and is being surfaced in its silvery aluminum cladding, while the steelwork of the south tower (at left) has reached only about half its full height, and still wears its reddish primer paint.

WOLFEN (1981) Seen here from the top of the Manhattan Bridge, where detectives played by Albert Finney and Diane Venora have climbed to interview an American Indian ironworker, the twin towers of the World Trade Center (along with the rest of the skyline) again stand as an emblem of urban culture in all its arrogance and (in the eyes of the titular man-beasts) decadence. By the time the film was made, in the early 1980s, the towers had so come to dominate the lower Manhattan skyline so firmly that it was almost impossible to imagine the city without them.

**OTHER PEOPLE'S MONEY
(1991).** In a view that has taken
on a poignancy unimaginable
when it was photographed
more than fifteen years ago,
the outrageous (but still
somehow appealing) mergers-
and-acquisitions wizard
Lawrence Garfield (Danny
DeVito) stands in front of the
towers of the World Trade
Center. In the film, the Garfield
character works out of an
office building at 40 Broad
Street, in the older financial
district a few blocks away.
But for the film's key publicity
image, the producers chose
the more imposing setting
of the Center's twin 110-story
towers, which by the early
1990s had come to be recog-
nized as the ultimate symbol
of global capitalism.

OVERLEAF Like the 1933 original,
the 1977 remake of KING
KONG was created largely in
Hollywood, using miniatures
and special effects. But for the
final scene, the producer Dino
de Laurentiis—with an eye
to publicity—decided to ship
his forty-foot-tall fabricated
creature across the country
in sections, re-assemble it on
the plaza of the World Trade
Center, and hold an "open
house" film shoot on the eve-
nings of June 21st-23rd, 1976.
Though the producers hoped
five thousand New Yorkers
would gather in the plaza
to serve as unpaid extras,
the first night only a fraction
of that number showed up.
Along the way, someone
managed to steal one of
Kong's artificial eyeballs,
forcing the art director to pull
a globe from a 5,000-watt
lamp, paint it appropriately,
and use it instead.

25TH HOUR (2002) In one of the first direct references to September 11th in a feature film, the director Spike Lee chose a window overlooking the ongoing recovery efforts at Ground Zero as the setting for a dispiriting exchange between Frank Slaughtery (Barry Pepper) and Jacob Elinsky (Philip Seymour Hoffman) about the prospects of their friend Monty Brogan (Edward Norton).

SPIKE LEE I told James Chinlund, the production designer, [that] I wanted to find an apartment, a location, where you look out the street and see directly into Ground Zero. So after numerous bogus locations we finally found this spot, and it's riveting looking out the window…. And once I looked out this window, I wanted to plan [the scene] in one take, one shot, just have Barry and Philip—two great actors—just deal with each other… and behind them have this large area of devastation.

…At the end of the [Ground Zero] scene you see some workers, with rakes in their hands, looking for human remains. That was their job. Some stupid journalist asked me, were those actors? Not actors. Everything we shot was real.

Spike Lee, director, *25th Hour*

THE STATE OF THE ART
LOCATION SHOOTING IN THE 1960s AND '70s

Filming NO WAY TO TREAT A LADY (1968) To film an extended conversation between a detective played by George Segal and an attractive woman who may be in danger, played by Lee Remick (here both represented by stand-ins), the cinematographer Jack Priestley (at center) needed to carry nearly a quarter-ton of equipment up into the floor of a city bus—including a Mitchell BNC camera, a "blimped"—or silenced— successor to the Mitchell NC (see opposite page) that alone weighed over 150 pounds.

Filming THE TAKING OF PELHAM ONE TWO THREE (1974) As location shooting became more popular, a new generation of directors and cinematographers began experimenting with lighter cameras and rigs that could render more fluidly the movement and dynamism of the city. In this view, a lightweight Arriflex BL camera has been attached with an aluminum rig and heavy-duty suction grips to the exterior of an actual New York City subway car, allowing the camera to move with the train as it pulls out of the station.

Filming COOGAN'S BLUFF (1968) Even as they first began moving into the streets and open spaces of the city, feature filmmakers continued to employ relatively heavy and static equipment, little different from that used in Hollywood. In this view, Clint Eastwood, playing Deputy Sheriff Walt Coogan, is filmed on motorcycle, pursuing a suspect through Fort Tryon Park near the northern tip of Manhattan. Atop the traditional wooden tripod mount is a Mitchell NC camera, the bulky but reliable workhorse of weekly newsreels.

Filming MIDNIGHT COWBOY (1969) By the late 1960s, **of the city in their location scenes. In this shot, filmed**

Winter shoot for an unidentified film. By the early 1970s, location crews were no longer a fair-weather phenomenon in New York City, but could be seen working around the year, even in the worst weather conditions.

JON KAMEN, PRODUCER New York [film crews] were forced to be more innovative. Just as you deal with other obstacles of living in New York, if you were to utilize these locations, you were just forced to be more innovative in the use of tools. You had to be a little lighter in terms of equipment, because it was vertical, you were moving into buildings. So that just like in everything else, from just the purely adaptive human instinct, we developed things here: dollies that were easier to use, simpler ways of laying track—you couldn't have the army of grips like you would have on the West Coast. A lot that happened here was purely out of survival, versus the luxury of the facilities of the West Coast. Things were a little more inventive, and the use of locations were more frequent because we didn't have as many studios—so it forced different techniques. It pushed filmmakers to locations 'cause you couldn't build as big a set. And we had locations, we had great locations....that would fit into the popular culture message of the aspirations of the city.

Filming TAXI DRIVER (1976)
Though location filming is often associated with a straight-forward, "documentary" style of lighting and camerawork, the director Martin Scorsese, making his first major feature in New York, sought to combine actual locations with a fluid, highly expressionistic use of camera movement. To achieve his vision, he and his cinematographer Michael Chapman employed a startling variety of equipment, including a motorized Chapman "Atlas" crane that would allow the camera to float dreamily above the sidewalk of East 12th Street and look down, in almost godlike manner, on the aftermath of the film's violent climax. To achieve the film's memorable shots of Travis Bickle (Robert De Niro) seen through the windshield of his cab as he moves around the city, the director Scorsese and Chapman mounted an Arriflex 35 BL camera to a platform bolted onto the chassis of a Checker cab; during shooting, the potholes proved so sizable that the camera jarred loose repeatedly, ruining shots and fraying tempers.

MICHAEL CHAPMAN, CINEMATOG-RAPHER, *TAXI DRIVER* For me, picking up on the animation of the city is a visual matter, seeing things happen. Witnessing an incident on a street corner. Watching the way a police-car turns, noticing when he puts the siren on and when he doesn't. It's constantly filling my head with ideas. With a sense of speed. With camera movement. That's very important to me.

HARLEM

I was thinking about how Harlem had a sense of urban Gothic to it. On Manhattan Avenue there are some structures that are beautiful. Look at European architecture and you see the same type of lines, the way the stone is cut. That's definitely evocative of the [film's] dark, sepia-toned mood.

Barry Michael Cooper, writer, *Sugar Hill*

ABOVE COTTON COMES TO HARLEM (1970) One of the first features to be shot on location in Harlem, the film attempts to connect to the district's storied past through scenes and characters such as this funeral director, dressed in an old-fashioned morning suit. In the distance, another now-vanished ritual is visible: an upended coal truck pouring a month's supply of heating coal into a tenement cellar.

ABOVE SUGAR HILL (1994) This dramatic night shoot offers a cross-section of Harlem's residential heritage: five-story masonry tenements fill the light-bathed foreground, while a high-rise postwar housing project twinkles in the distance. **OPPOSITE PAGE** Ironically, though the film was shot extensively in Harlem, none of it took place in Sugar Hill itself, a stretch of imposing apartment houses and townhouses along the ridge of Edgecombe Avenue, overlooking the Harlem Valley.

WYNN THOMAS, PRODUCTION DESIGNER, *MALCOLM X* The important thing for us was trying to recreate a little bit of the [historical] reality. Streetlights and signage and trash cans and cars were all very different then. What we're trying to do is recreate the time period.

MALCOLM X (1992) **With scrupulous attention to detail, the director Spike Lee and his production designer Wynn Thomas recreated an early 1960s political rally—featuring the controversial minister and activist Malcolm X (Denzel Washington)—in the same spot where the actual event occurred, on the north side of 125th Street, adjacent to the Apollo Theater, Harlem's best-known cultural landmark.**

NEW YORK MOMENTS
1966–1975

OPPOSITE **THE PANIC IN NEEDLE PARK** (1971) **Directed by Jerry Schatzberg from a script by Joan Didion and John Gregory Dunne, the film offers a sympathetic portrayal of two young drug addicts trying to survive on the streets of New York. In this scene, Helen (Kitty Winn) leans close to Bobby (Al Pacino), after trimming his hair on a Manhattan rooftop.**

LEFT **KLUTE** (1971) **John Klute (Donald Sutherland) and Bree Daniels (Jane Fonda) share a tender moment as they shop for groceries at a sidewalk bodega on Ninth Avenue in the 40s, around the corner from Bree's walk-up apartment.**

SHAFT (1971) As the opening titles roll, the maverick detective John Shaft (Richard Roundtree) walks into moving traffic at Seventh Avenue and 42nd Street, correcting the impression of a motorist who assumes he has the right-of-way. According to Roundtree, the director Gordon Parks instructed the actor to stride down the sidewalk and into the actual traffic on Seventh Avenue— with no stunt drivers or cars employed—capturing the results from cameras positioned in vantage points all around the intersection.

THE PRISONER OF SECOND AVENUE (1975) Leaning out her apartment balcony (located in fact on Second Avenue, at 87th Street) a frustrated housewife named Edna Edison (Anne Bancroft) makes her feelings known to a neighbor upstairs.

JEREMY (1973) **In a classic ritual of adolescent courtship in New York, two students at a performing arts high school in Manhattan— Jeremy Jones (Robby Benson) and Susan Rollins (Glynnis O'Connor)—meander aimlessly through Central Park as their relationship gradually blossoms.**

Who do you want? No one gets in, unless I know who they want. I'm the concierge. My husband used to be the concierge, but he's dead. Now I'm the concierge.

Madelyn Cates in *The Producers*

THE PRODUCERS (1968)

On a tenement stoop on "West Jane Street"—actually the East 80s—the producer Max Bialystock and his partner Leo Bloom (Zero Mostel and Gene Wilder), run the formidable gauntlet of the "concierge" (Madelyn Cates) guarding the building's front door.

ANNIE HALL
SATURDAY NIGHT FEVER
MANHATTAN
GHOSTBUSTERS
DESPERATELY SEEKING SUSAN
TAXI DRIVER
FAME
NIGHTHAWKS
DOWNTOWN 81
THE BONFIRE OF THE VANITIES
FORT APACHE, THE BRONX
WOLFEN
JUMPIN' AT THE BONEYARD
I LIKE IT LIKE THAT
THE ANDERSON TAPES
SPLASH
MEN IN BLACK
THE WARRIORS
THE PICKLE
CRUISING
HAIR
RAGTIME
AN UNMARRIED WOMAN
DESPERATELY SEEKING SUSAN
KRAMER VS. KRAMER
BROADWAY DANNY ROSE
MY DINNER WITH ANDRÉ
TIMES SQUARE
THE BROTHER FROM ANOTHER PLANET

Pulses fluttered, gaiety arose, and New Yorkers said they were living in the biggest backlot in the world. New York would no longer be Hollywood on the Hudson; Los Angeles would be New York on the Pacific.

John Corry, *New York Times*, 1978

JOHN CORRY, *NEW YORK TIMES*, 1978 In the next few months, about a dozen movies will be made here, and while no one can say what will happen after that, it is possible that this year the movie business will be ever more wondrous than it was last. The movie people did many wondrous things last year, but the most wondrous is that they are supposed to have spent $100 million in New York while they made their movies. Nothing like that has ever happened before.

TAXI DRIVER (1976) The film's notorious shoot in July 1975 was marked not only by mid-summer weather that some compared to a sub-tropical rain forest—long stretches of steamy heat punctuated by torrential downpours—but by bizarre and random acts of violence nearby. While scouting locations around Lincoln Center, crew members saw a large man punch an old woman in the mouth for no apparent reason, while during the filming of a scene in which Travis Bickle (Robert De Niro) kills a mugger in an Upper West Side bodega, a real murder occurred around the corner at Columbus Avenue and 86th Street. "We didn't know which cops were for us," the director Martin Scorsese later recalled, "and which were for the real killing around the corner. Everything got mixed together and we really couldn't tell, so we just shot whatever was happening around us."

Someday a real rain will come and wash all the scum off the streets.

Robert De Niro (as Travis Bickle) in *Taxi Driver*

MARTIN SCORSESE, DIRECTOR, *TAXI DRIVER* That summer was a down point for New York, and it shows in that film, in the mood of it. It was so hot you could see the violence shimmering in the air, taste it in your mouth, and there we were in the middle of it.

Annie Hall's apartment was on 70th Street between Lexington and Park, which is my favorite block in the city. Great architecture, and it hasn't been ruined.

Woody Allen, director, *Annie Hall*

ANNIE HALL (1977) Unlike the crowds his films would attract in later years, few passers-by in the summer of 1976 paid any attention to a scene being shot by the director Woody Allen on East 68th Street, between Park and Madison Avenues, in which a Brooklyn-born comedian named Alvy Singer (Allen) and Annie Hall (Diane Keaton), a would-be singer from Chippewa Falls, Wisconsin, have their first awkward conversation.

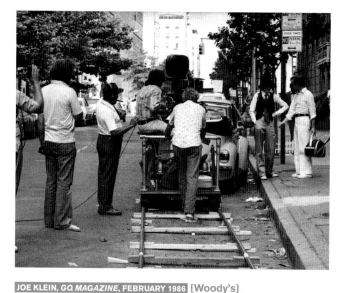

JOE KLEIN, *GQ MAGAZINE*, FEBRUARY 1986 [Woody's] city commingles with the real one, especially on warm, sunny days in autumn and spring, on West Side movie lines, at parties where someone is talking too loud, in delis and in cabarets where standards are sung. The rest of us notice it from time to time—"This is a Woody Allen kind of moment"—but it is his fantasy, and, one imagines, he inhabits it as fully as the heroine of *The Purple Rose of Cairo* inhabits hers.

BRIAN HAMILL, STILL PHOTOGRAPHER, *ANNIE HALL* When you work on something special, as I knew this would be...I didn't know it was going to be quite as big as it was, but I knew it was a special movie, a very special movie.

(1977) The movie's opening scene—John Travolta (as Tony Manero) strutting down a sidewalk to the music of the Bee Gees—was also the first to be filmed. Working on location on Fourth Avenue and 86th Street in Bay Ridge, Brooklyn, the film crew was astonished to see hundreds of local fans who had gathered to catch a glimpse of the fast-rising star.

FAME (1980) For the film's title number—in which students spill out of the city's High School for Performing Arts and perform an impromptu dance routine among midtown traffic, the filmmakers arranged with the Mayor's Office of Film, Theatre and Broadcasting to close 46th Street for four days in the summer of 1979. The actual Performing Arts school building—now home to the Jacqueline Kennedy Onassis High School—was located on the left side of the street, out of sight, while the structure presented in the film as the school, on the right side, was actually a decommissioned church.

ALAN PARKER, DIRECTOR, FAME This scene is pushing reality to the very edge. Could it have happened?…It could happen, but obviously I'm cheating a little in regards to seeing this in the middle of 46th Street in New York—it was one time when I pushed things to the edge of its theatrical, musical genre.

There are all kinds of ways to shoot the city of New York. In the case of *Manhattan*, the concept was to lay the picture out in what I call "romantic reality."

Gordon Willis, cinematographer, *Manhattan*

THE NEW YORKER, SEPTEMBER 1977 [The cinematographer Gordon Willis, the director Woody Allen], and the chief cameraman are crouching on the shadowy sidewalk now, about a third of the way up the block from the bench. They take turns looking through the director's viewfinder; they talk, point, agree. A chalk mark is set at their feet…a dolly is rolled up to the chalk mark; [first assistant cameraman] Jimmy Hovey sets a Panavision camera on the dolly and—turning a wheel—raises the camera to the proper height. Willis instructs him to put on a 75-mm. anamorphic lens; then Hovey attaches a loaded film magazine to the top of the camera. All four men stand up. Through the camera's viewer are now framed—in the small, black-bordered rectangle that has the same proportions as a Panavision screen (2.35 to 1)—the street leading to the bench; the bench; the street lamp next to it; a concrete tub of flowers; the railing; part of the Queensboro Bridge; and the unpredictable sky. Except for the lights and the horizon, everything is gray.

MANHATTAN (1978) An all-night walk conversation between Isaac Davis (Woody Allen) and Mary Wilkie (Diane Keaton) comes to an end in this memorable scene, which was shot at the foot of 58th Street, overlooking the East River and the Queensboro Bridge, at around four a.m.—just before dawn—on the morning of August 14th, 1978. Except for the string lights on the bridge, which the filmmakers arranged with the city to leave on, and the street lamp, which they arranged to turn off, the scene was shot entirely with available light.

GHOSTBUSTERS (1984)
Even before they do battle with their supernatural foes, the team (from left to right, Ernie Hudson, Bill Murray, Dan Aykroyd and Harold Ramis) must survive a frightening eruption of the street bed in front of "550 Central Park West"—actually 55 Central Park West, a handsome 1930 Art Deco apartment house at the corner of 66th Street. Giant broken slabs, placed atop the actual street surface, created the illusion of the pavement being pushed up from below.

SIGOURNEY WEAVER, ACTOR, *GHOSTBUSTERS* The crowd of extras we had for the *Ghostbusters* movies—man, that was a lot of energy. Those people would stay up all night in the freezing cold, screaming "Ghostbusters!" It made you proud to be a New Yorker.

HAROLD RAMIS, CO-WRITER/ACTOR, *GHOSTBUSTERS* When we shot all the stuff in all the different locations around the city…the legend over the weeks started to grow, because people would see this ambulance tearing around the city, they'd see us in our uniforms, and say, "what the hell?" "Ghostbusters," that's all we'd say.

SUSAN SEIDELMAN, DIRECTOR, *DESPERATELY SEEKING SUSAN* Since I came from the independent…New York movie scene, I knew a bunch of…downtown characters who were performing in these low-budget movies that probably no one on the West Coast had ever—or will ever—see. So I brought those people to the equation [of the film], people like Richard Hell, who had been one of the leads in *Smithereens*, and Rockets Redglare, and Richard Edson. And, in a sense, Madonna was also coming from that New York downtown world.

SUSAN SEIDELMAN The filming was…ten weeks [in total]. Somewhere probably around the sixth or seventh week, people were beginning to notice Madonna and the filming, and suddenly there were issues of security. In the beginning of the film, when we first filmed with Madonna on St. Mark's Place, we didn't have police guards or any extra security; later in the film we needed to have some extra security put on because—it was amazing to witness—literally in that time span from start of filming to end of filming, the level of Madonna awareness had jumped enormously.

119

NEW YORK LANDMARKS
1976–1985

TAXI DRIVER (1976) For the director Martin Scorsese, the use of actual locations worked to ground the movie's stylized—sometimes almost phantasmagorical—texture in the mundane realities of a city cabbie's existence. In this view, Travis Bickle (Robert De Niro, on far right) shares a late-night coffee with fellow drivers (including Peter Boyle, second from left) in the BELLMORE CAFETERIA at Park Avenue South and 28th Street, an all-night eatery favored by New York cab drivers for decades until its closing, in the early 1980s, to make way for an apartment house.

JAMES WOLCOTT, 1997 Watching *Taxi Driver* today, one is aware of how much the midtown urbanscape has changed for the better since then. We're not used to improvement in New York—it takes some mental adjusting. Yet it's undeniable: Times Square is no longer the carny Sodom of midnight cowboys....Most of the porn theaters and fleabag hotels are as extinct now as the Automats and pawnshops of 40s noirs. The cabbie hangout in the film, the Bellmore Cafeteria...closed years ago. Travis Bickle's New York has become a historical figment.

WOODY ALLEN, WRITER/DIRECTOR, *ANNIE HALL* I have an affectionate view of Manhattan; I've only seen it as an extremely exciting, wonderful, romantic place, ever since I was taken here as a child. It's sort of automatic with me; any time I make a picture in Manhattan, that's the way I see the city. If Martin Scorsese makes a picture of the city, it gets filtered through a different view, but any time I do it, it comes out this way.

ANNIE HALL (1977) **By setting his unfolding romance before a series of photogenic urban landmarks, Allen quietly reminded filmgoers—including New Yorkers themselves— that despite its social and economic woes, mid-1970s New York retained an extraordinary physical heritage. Stepping out onto Pier 11 in the East River—now the site of the South Street Seaport— Alvy and Annie (Woody Allen and Diane Keaton) declare their feelings for each other in a shot framed by the** BROOKLYN BRIDGE, **perhaps the city's greatest symbol of human connection.**

FAME (1980) After reviewing an early script, the city's Board of Education refused to allow *Fame* to be shot in its actual setting, the High School of Performing Arts, claiming that the film would "paint too dark a picture" of the school, and insisting that New York high school students did not use the kind of language represented in the screenplay. The Mayor's Office of Film, Theatre and Broadcasting came to the rescue by suggesting an alternative location: the former HAAREN HIGH SCHOOL, whose 1906 Flemish Revival building at 59th Street and Tenth Avenue (empty at the time, and since renovated to become John Jay College of Criminal Justice) proved an ideal environment for the film's interior scenes, such as the ballet classes and practice sessions shown here.

ALAN PARKER, DIRECTOR, *FAME* New York is very easy for shooting with regard to permissions, because unlike London, New York has a whole Mayor's department to look after filmmakers, and they were incredibly helpful to me.

MANHATTAN (1978) Taking advantage of the cinematographer Gordon Willis's dramatic backlighting for a scene at a summer benefit at the MUSEUM OF MODERN ART, the still photographer Brian Hamill took this striking view of Woody Allen and Diane Keaton. "If you don't get good stills on a Gordon Willis movie," Hamill later observed, "then you're not doing your job properly."

OPPOSITE In NIGHTHAWKS (1981) the ROOSEVELT ISLAND TRAMWAY— proposed in the 1970s as an innovative way to connect the island's new residential community to midtown Manhattan—became the setting for a dramatic scene in which a terrorist (Rutger Hauer) grabs control of a tram car and takes its passengers hostage. In this shot, a detective named DaSilva (Sylvester Stallone) uses a helicopter to peer into the car, which dangles motionless above the East River.

BELOW DOWNTOWN 81 (1981) Originally known as *New York Beat*, the film follows a poor New York artist—played by the 21 year-old painter Jean-Michel Basquiat, whose meteoric career would later be the subject of its own feature film (page 187)—on a picaresque journey around the city, including a stop at Frank Lloyd Wright's 1959 GUGGENHEIM MUSEUM.

THE BRONX

FORT APACHE, THE BRONX (1981) Patrolmen Murphy and Correlli (Paul Newman and Ken Wahl) capture two suspects on a South Bronx rooftop. The film sparked an angry response during its production from community activists and local elected officials, opposed to its portrait of the area as an unrelieved wasteland. In the end, the filmmakers refused to alter their portrayal, but agreed to provide a modest disclaimer at the start of the film.

Filming THE BONFIRE OF THE VANITIES (1990) Working under the elevated tracks of the subway, cameramen shoot a Bronx avenue from atop a Chapman crane. Like *Fort Apache, the Bronx*, the movie courted controversy during its shooting, when Borough President Fernando Ferrer publicly called on the filmmakers to balance their dark portrait of the Bronx with "positive images" of the borough. Except for a few headlines, nothing came of the criticism.

LEFT WOLFEN (1981) To provide a suitable home for the film's supernatural, wolf-like creatures, production designer Paul Sylbert built an abandoned church—at the time the largest exterior set ever created for a New York film—on the rubble-filled blocks around Charlotte Street and East 172nd Street, in the very heart of the arson-driven devastation that swept through the South Bronx in the late 1970s. In this view, detectives played by Albert Finney and Diane Venora wander the rubble-lined streets, looking for clues. **BELOW** While shooting on location in 1979, the filmmakers captured—and included in the film—shots of actual burned-out tenement buildings being imploded into rubble.

DAVID VIDAL, *NEW YORK TIMES*, NOVEMBER 3, 1979 A major construction effort of the kind Charlotte Street has been unable to obtain in real life is proceeding, in the unreal work of the movies, on one of the most barren sites in the Bronx. Shipments of rubble have been brought in for scenic effects, but garbage that has been accumulating there has been removed.

Filming JUMPIN' AT THE BONEYARD (1992) Following two troubled brothers (Tim Roth and Alexis Arquette) as they try to make sense of their lives on a daylong journey across the Bronx to reunite with their mother, Jeff Stanzler's film encompassed a wide variety of locations in the borough—including dozens of burned-out blocks (such as the one in this view) that remained visible long after the borough's epidemic of arson and abandonment had subsided.

This area gave me my youth.

Darnell Martin, writer/director, *I Like It Like That*

I LIKE IT LIKE THAT (1994)
A strikingly different vision of the Bronx was visible in Darnell Martin's film, set on East 170th Street in Morrisania, a Latino district whose impoverished but vibrant streets serve as an outdoor stage for the quarrels and reconciliations of the film's main characters, including Lisette (Lauren Vélez, in black shirt at center), her husband Chino (Jon Seda, at right), and her mother Rosaria (Rita Moreno, in middle distance).

LOCATION STUNTS AND TRICKS

THE ANDERSON TAPES
(1971) A stunt man playing a NYPD tactical patrolman swings across to a luxurious Fifth Avenue apartment building that has been broken into—and taken over—by a team of professional burglars. For its exteriors, the director Sidney Lumet used the former Otto Kahn mansion at 1 East 91st Street, a massive Italian Renaissance-style palazzo that is now home to the Convent of the Sacred Heart.

HUDSON HAWK (1991)
Bruce Willis, playing the title
character, races out of control
on a hospital gurney down the
ramp of the Brooklyn Bridge.
To facilitate the shoot, the
Mayor's Office of Film, Theatre
and Broadcasting arranged for
the bridge's eastbound lanes
to be closed to traffic for six
consecutive nights.

SPLASH (1984) In the film's
climactic moment, stunt-
woman Erin O'Neil, doubling
for Darryl Hannah, dives off
Pier 17 into the East River
—after receiving hepatitis
shots to prevent infection.
For other scenes in the film,
O'Neil swam the city's rivers
and bays wearing a mermaid
suit—a 35 lb. appliance made
of urethane "skinflex" panels
joined together with Krazy
Glue. The costume was so
realistic that pilot fish, who
generally swim only along
other fish, came up beside her
in the water.

OPPOSITE **Filming** MEN IN BLACK (1997) **In order to shoot a brief sequence in which Will Smith, playing "Agent J," is sent flying backwards by the recoil of his powerful alien pistol, elaborate stunt equipment was installed on MacDougal Street in SoHo. Smith is pulled by a winched steel cable, attached to a harness placed under his suit (and later eliminated digitally from the film), toward a safety mattress that cushions his fall.**

THIS PAGE **Filming** "CROCODILE" DUNDEE II (1988) **In order to shoot this scene—in which a villain clinging to the side of a skyscraper is greeted by the title character (Paul Hogan), strolling insouciantly along the precipitous ledge— filmmakers set up a wooden deck a few feet below the building's fifteenth-floor, serving as a platform for the camera as well as protection for the performers.**

CONEY ISLAND

DARREN ARONOFSKY, SCREENWRITER/DIRECTOR, *REQUIEM FOR A DREAM*

I grew up about five miles from Coney Island, and Coney Island was always the forbidden world...it was kind of dangerous but it was also extremely fun, because of the amusement park—and also beautiful, because of the aesthetic of it. And for years I've...been feeding off of it artistically, and it's just really influenced me as a filmmaker. So when I had the chance to move this film from the Bronx [where the original Hugh Selby, Jr. novel had been set] to Coney Island—and Selby didn't mind, Selby was like, yeah, it's the same culture—I was really...excited to sort of bring it home. So all these locations in this movie are locations from my youth...Everything from where the yentas hang out to the handball courts—it's all very personal.

ANNIE HALL (1977) **To portray the childhood scenes of Woody Allen's alter ego, Alvy Singer (played here as a nine-year-old by Jonathan Munk), the film-makers employed actual Coney Island locations, which (carefully framed, and filled with a few period details, such as the pair of sailors in this view) evoked a powerful sense of the wartime years not so much as they actually transpired, but as they might be recalled, decades later, in memory.**

THE WARRIORS (1979) **The decrepit but still somehow picturesque landscape of 1970s Coney Island provided the home base from which the Warriors, a street gang, venture out at the start of the film—and to which, after an epic journey to the northern Bronx, they return wearily the following morning.**

ABOVE AND PREVIOUS REQUIEM FOR A DREAM (2000) Darren Aronofsky's intense, highly stylized film moves among several parts of oceanside Brooklyn, from the familiar community of older Jewish women of Brighton Beach, to the toxic underworld of young drug-addicts in Coney Island's flophouses, to the eerie, literally dreamlike environment that links the two—the endless wooden boardwalk and the infinite sea it overlooks.

BRITTANY MURPHY (AS MOLLY GUNN) IN *UPTOWN GIRLS* Everyone was talking and I couldn't understand a word they were saying and then their voices became a blur and soon I couldn't even recognize their faces, they were like these blobs…and I knew I had to run away. So I packed my knapsack, got on the train, and looked up at the map and decided I wanted to live on Coney Island. I thought it would be, you know, a real island.

UPTOWN GIRLS (2003) Trying to recapture the magic she had discovered there as a child, the adult Molly Gunn (Brittany Murphy) brings eight-year-old Ray Schleine (Dakota Fanning) to Coney Island (LEFT)—only to find the park's attractions closed for the season, and struggling to sustain a festive air amidst a bleak landscape of high-rise projects. But when Ray makes her own nighttime flight to the park (ABOVE), at the film's climax, the surroundings melt away and we see an environment that, for all its mundane encroachments, still seems to offer the possibility of a magical escape from the world.

BACKLIT STREET

MARY HARRON, DIRECTOR, *AMERICAN PSYCHO* The scene shows Christian Bale [as the leading character Patrick Bateman] striding through an alleyway towards a homeless man whom he later kills. We had a bunch of lights and a big old smoke machine and it looked great, very modern Jack-the-Ripper. It's supposed to be near Wall Street but I believe it's actually an alleyway in Chinatown. The only period dressing we did was to add piles of garbage and some graffiti. The street scenes had to be done in New York—there is just no substitute. It's very difficult to make any other city stand in because New York is dense and vertical, and it has architectural details all its own.

With the growing popularity of location shooting in New York arose one of the most iconic (if not indeed cliché) images of the contemporary city: a glistening wet street by night, filled with a mysterious shroud of fog or vapor, backlit by an intense (but unseen) light source casting long, eerie shadows across the scene. OPPOSITE PAGE AMERICAN

PSYCHO (2000) A backlit alley in Chinatown. RIGHT A PERFECT MURDER (1998) A backlit street in Long Island City. BELOW STATE OF GRACE (1990) A backlit parking lot in Hell's Kitchen. (See pages 152 and 225 for other backlit New York streets.)

CENTRAL PARK

THE APRIL FOOLS (1969) Central Park's special place within the city—a world apart, yet located in the very heart of Manhattan—has long encouraged its use as a setting for special, transformative moments in the lives of filmic characters. In this view, on a rainy spring day, Jack Lemmon and Catherine Deneuve share the early days of a love affair amidst the empty benches of the Naumburg bandshell, one of the many elements within its landscape that make Central Park a kind of "city" unto itself.

UP THE SANDBOX (1972)
Another of the park's attractions, the Carousel, frames a different kind of transformative moment in the last scene of *Up the Sandbox*. Finding her husband Paul (Paul Selby) riding the wooden horses with their two young children,

Margaret (Barbra Streisand) announces to him a third child is on the way—then hails a taxi, and leaves him.

CRUISING (1979) **For much of the 20th century, Central Park by night provided a tacitly accepted site for homosexual liaisons, forbidden by law in most other public spaces of the city. In *Cruising*, Al Pacino— playing an undercover police- man posing as a gay man, in order to catch a murderer— wanders the park's deserted, after-hours pathways.**

THE OUT-OF-TOWNERS (1970) **It was one of the crueler ironies of New York's troubles in the late 1960s and early '70s that Central Park—always intended as a peaceful refuge from the city—gained widespread notoriety (deserved or not) as the most dangerous place in the city. That reputation, still at its height, was invoked in this sequence from *The Out-of-Towners,* in which a pair of hapless visitors from suburban Ohio, George and Gwen Kellerman (Sandy Dennis and Jack Lemmon), are forced to spend the night in the forbidding landscape.**

LEFT AND ABOVE HAIR (1979)
The film adaptation of the celebrated Broadway musical used Central Park as its primary setting, in part to soften the inevitable anachronisms of a show about the 1960s being produced on the eve of the '80s, but also to take advantage of the intrinsic "counter-culture" of the park itself, a utopian landscape set apart from the commercial city. Within the park's 843 acres, the filmmakers found a universe of settings—including a spring festival, set on the Sheep Meadow almost ten years to the day after the actual "Be-in" (the mass gathering that inspired the scene) that took place in March 1967, in exactly the same location.

SIX DEGREES OF SEPA-RATION (1993) **Envisioned initially as an Arcadian foil to the stratified, class-bound city around it, Central Park provides a strangely appropriate setting for Paul (Will Smith), an imaginative con man and fantasist who survives hand-to-mouth in its open landscape. In this scene he manages to convince two credulous out-of-towners (Heather Graham and Erik Thal) that he is actually the illegitimate, disinherited son of a wealthy art dealer whose apartment overlooks the park.**

OPPOSITE PAGE ONE FINE DAY (1996) **Another longstanding mission of the park—as a place where jaded city-dwellers might be reminded of life's simpler pleasures—is brought to life in this scene of two sophisticated divorcees, Jack Taylor and Melanie Parker (George Clooney and Michelle Pfeiffer) reliving the joys of splashing through puddles as they race with their kids through the park.**

HISTORIC RECREATIONS

OPPOSITE PAGE **THE NIGHT THEY RAIDED MINSKY'S (1968)** The first musical to be shot entirely in New York, the film transformed East 26th Street, between First and Second Avenues, into the setting of Minsky's, the famed Manhattan burlesque house. Lovingly recreating East Houston Street in 1925, the set included accurate historic prices in the shop windows, and a police precinct house from which to carry out the climactic "raid." When demolition work for nearby Bellevue Hospital threatened to drown out the filming, Mayor Lindsay personally arranged for the wrecking crews to shut their jackhammers and bulldozers while the cameras rolled. Soon the shoot became a tourist attraction, covered by local television and radio stations and photographed by countless visitors.

My heart was really in the Little Italy sequences, in the old streets of New York, the music, all that turn-of-the-century atmosphere.

Francis Ford Coppola, director, *The Godfather, Part II*

LEFT AND ABOVE THE GODFATHER, PART II (1974) To portray the world in which young Vito Corleone (Robert De Niro) changes from an "honorable grocer's clerk" (BELOW) into a ruthless mobster, the director Francis Ford Coppola (LEFT) and his production designer Dean Tavoularis painstakingly redressed East Sixth Street, near Avenue A, to appear as it might have in 1917. The transformation included removing all sidewalk parking meters (which were quickly replaced after the shoot) and replacing the block's existing street signs with period signs, reproduced from historic photographs in the Traffic Department's archives.

RAGTIME (1981)
Commandeering 11th Street between Avenues A and B, Ragtime's designer Patrizia van Brandenstein evoked the dense and crowded streets of the Lower East Side in 1906.

PATRIZIA VON BRANDENSTEIN, PRODUCTION DESIGNER, *RAGTIME*
Eleventh between A and B—that was our block. Because the East Village had not yet been [the site of] high-rise development—as of course it is now—we were able to get full vista, looking east and west, and uptown and downtown, so that although the street itself has a claustrophobic feel, the east and west vistas open out. What [we see] is real. No mattes. No mattes. I don't think it could be done today.

When you're in a street that's blocked off [to make a period film], then you're really in the world, so you really feel like you're in a place that doesn't exist any more. For me, the experience of shooting the film... walking around in that world... was the ultimate thrill.

Brad Dourif, actor, *Ragtime*

RAGTIME (1981) In the film, Elizabeth McGovern plays Evelyn Nesbit, an actual historical figure today remembered mostly for her role in the romantic triangle that led to the murder of architect Stanford White. Paying a surprising visit to the impoverished area, she lingers as a sidewalk peddler played by Mandy Patimkin shapes a silhouette portrait of her. (His four-year-old daughter is played by Jenny Nichols, the daughter of the director Mike Nichols.)

SLEEPERS (1996) To portray the adolescent world from which its four main characters will grow into a life of crime and revenge, the filmmakers redressed several blocks in Greenpoint, Brooklyn to stand in for Hell's Kitchen, to the west of midtown Manhattan, circa 1966. The film carefully captures the texture of New York neighborhood life in that era, surprisingly little changed from decades earlier: broad, low-rise avenues filled with period cars and buses, the corner candy store and soda cart, and a game of stickball being played on a dead-end block that is intended to represent West 47th Street, leading down to Pier 87.

SOHO

I remember the cobblestones that we were walking on, and the streets…That really was a romantic scene.

Jill Clayburgh, actor, *An Unmarried Woman*

Once blocks of abandoned warehouses, this area in the 1960s was taken over by artists attracted by the lower rents who converted these buildings, many of them with magnificent grilled fronts, into galleries and lofts. Now SoHo is a mandatory stop for the tourist buses which unload women from the suburbs for an afternoon's walking tour of the galleries and lunch at reasonably priced restaurants serving the best of health foods.

AN UNMARRIED WOMAN (1978) To frame the relationship of a recently separated uptown woman (Jill Clayburgh) and a successful downtown painter (Alan Bates), Paul Mazursky's film took audiences to a part of the city that had rarely appeared on screen: SoHo, a grimy industrial district filled with 19th century cast-iron loft buildings, that had been reborn in the 1970s as capital of the contemporary art world. Scenes shot by day on Greene Street reveal the blue-collar activities that had defined the area for over a century—but would disappear almost entirely in the following decade or so—while those filmed on Mercer Street at night show the hauntingly empty streetscapes that would also start to vanish within a few years, as galleries, bars, restaurants, and clubs began filling the area.

JILL CLAYBURGH, ACTOR God, that was a different SoHo. That was a really different SoHo. It's hard to believe that SoHo existed where it was all artists…but it did. In that short a time—I mean it's really not that long a time—boy, has that changed!

AFTER HOURS (1985) **Directed by Martin Scorsese in the summer of 1984, the film was intended to evoke the SoHo of a decade earlier, when the district had not yet become a lively center of downtown life. In this view, Griffin Dunne, as a bewildered outsider from uptown, tries to make his way home among the dark, empty, forbidding streets.**

MICHAEL BALLHAUS, CINEMATOGRAPHER, *AFTER HOURS* It was a very strange world there, but exciting. It was not glamorous. It was just, you know, dirty, down and dirty, and [the film] showed all the different characters, the clubs and everything, and all the weirdness that happened in that area.

MARTIN SCORSESE, DIRECTOR, *AFTER HOURS* It had a perfect setting [for a rapid, eight-week shooting schedule]: it's SoHo in the middle of the night. There's nobody there. Everybody's in these lofts, or in nightclubs. Something's going on but it ain't happening in the street—the streets are empty. You can light three or four blocks, do two takes, and move on.

**HANNAH AND HER SISTERS
(1986) Even as SoHo's
transformation from industrial
district to artistic center
proceeded, its next stage
of evolution—to an upscale
retail and residential
neighborhood—was already
well under way. In this view,
Michael Caine, attempting
a "casual" encounter with
his wife's sister (Barbara
Hershey), runs past one of
the expensive boutiques
that had begun to dot the
area by the mid-1980s.**

**PRIME (2005) Perhaps no
single setting suggests the
stylish consumer culture
that in recent years has
come to define SoHo better
than Dean & Deluca, the
vast specialty food store
on Prince Street in which
Prime's romantic lead,
Rafi Gardet (Uma Thurman)
is shopping just before
a crucial run-in with
her ex-boyfriend, David
(Bryan Greenberg).**

NEW YORK MOMENTS
1976–1985

DESPERATELY SEEKING SUSAN (1985) In an amusing, character-defining moment, Susan (Madonna), arriving at the uptown Port Authority Bus Terminal on 181st Street, prepares for her entrance to the city by using the restroom's hand dryer in an unconventional way—a moment that the actress improvised on the spot.

KRAMER VS. KRAMER (1979)

The transformation of Ted Kramer (Dustin Hoffman) from a career-obsessed ad man into a caring, attentive father—after his wife of many years has abruptly left him—is played out in this abiding ritual of family life in the city: accompanying a young child to elementary school, and helping tie his shoes. The widely admired acting gifts of Justin Henry, who played Kramer's son, were especially crucial during the shooting of this scene at P.S. 6 on Madison Avenue, during which the young actor's friends and fellow students— he actually attended the same school—were taunting him, just beyond camera range.

BROADWAY DANNY ROSE
(1984) For decades, veteran show-business figures have gathered at the "comedians' table" at the Carnegie Deli (at Seventh Avenue and 55th Street) to regale each other with jokes, anecdotes, and stories—a nightly ritual that Woody Allen chose as the narrative frame for his epic tale of a hapless talent agent, Danny Rose. Among the real comedians who appeared in the film as table regulars are Sandy Baron, Corbett Monica, Jackie Gayle, Will Jordan, and Morty Gunty.

MY DINNER WITH ANDRÉ
(1981) A familiar irony in the life of young, aspiring New Yorkers is brought out in this scene of Wally Shawn, a struggling playwright, riding the graffiti-scarred subway to reach his elegant, expensive dinner with a legendary theatrical director, André Bishop.

**THE BROTHER FROM
ANOTHER PLANET** (1984)
Crash-landing into New York
Bay and making landfall
at a ghostly Ellis Island,
the mute, otherworldly
"immigrant" (Joe Morton)
in John Sayles' film is soon
removed by a Park Service
boat to Manhattan, where,
like millions before him, he
will struggle to make his way
in a frightening, unfamiliar
world. "It's basically a fable
that takes place in hard
reality," observed Ernest
Dickerson, the cinematographer of the film.

"CROCODILE" DUNDEE
BIG
WALL STREET
WORKING GIRL
DO THE RIGHT THING
WHEN HARRY MET SALLY…
WALL STREET
SIX DEGREES OF SEPARATION
THE FISHER KING
SINGLE WHITE FEMALE
SMOKE
BLUE IN THE FACE
CLOCKERS
SOPHIE'S CHOICE
CHASING AMY
IT COULD HAPPEN TO YOU
LITTLE MANHATTAN
MEAN STREETS
*batteries not included
CROOKLYN
WARRIORS
I LIKE IT LIKE THAT
GOODFELLAS
CROSSING DELANCEY
MO' BETTER BLUES
THE PROFESSIONAL
JUNGLE FEVER

The streets of New York have a richness you can't duplicate anywhere. There's a sense of commotion. It's not the buildings, but the people you see walking by.
Susan Seidelman, director

New Yorkers may enjoy pretending to be unaffected by celebrities, but there are still plenty of them out there willing to wait an hour or two or three on a Friday or Saturday night—arms full of packages, briefcases in hand—for the chance to gaze at a movie star....Even for the most jaded Manhattanites, there's a strange satisfaction in seeing a star's face assume human proportions (and, if it is a glamorous face, display human flaws). For out-of-towners...glimpsing a star up close may be a cherished souvenir long after the Big Apple ashtrays are broken. And it's free.

1986–1995

LEFT **"CROCODILE" DUNDEE (1986)** Bringing his outback instincts to the wilds of midtown Manhattan, Michael J. "Crocodile" Dundee (Paul Hogan) climbs a lamppost to better survey the terrain of Fifth Avenue.

RIGHT BIG (1988) **F.A.O. Schwarz's vast toy store on Fifth Avenue—a landmark for generations of New York children—provided the setting for the fondly remembered scene in which Robert Loggia, a toy company executive making weekend rounds, joins Tom Hanks—a 13-year-old boy inhabiting the body of a man—in a spirited duet on a giant electronic keyboard. Though most of the displays were those found in the actual store, the overscaled keyboard was added by the film's production designer, Santo Loquasto, as a way to subtly reinforce the movie's underlying confusion of big and small.**

162

WALL STREET (1987)

Looking out on the towers of lower Manhattan from his well-appointed lair (an actual office space at Broadway and Vesey Street, redressed for the film) the ruthless financial titan Gordon Gekko (Michael Douglas) carries out his unending stream of lucrative, high-powered deals.

WORKING GIRL (1988) Seen from the deck of the Staten Island Ferry, crossing the upper bay, those same downtown towers take on the quality of an enchanted city for **Tess McGill (Melanie Griffith),** an office worker from Staten Island who dreams of entering the loftier precincts of the business world.

WHEN HARRY MET SALLY…
(1989) One of the most
memorable location scenes in
the city's history was filmed
at Katz's Delicatessen at 205
East Houston Street, featuring Meg Ryan, Billy Crystal,
and a customer played by the
mother of the film's director,
Rob Reiner. "Meg just sat
there panting for about eight
or ten hours," the screenwriter
Nora Ephron later recalled, "I
don't know how many takes
Rob did. She did it over, and
over, and over, and over."
"Every time they had to do
another camera angle," the
deli's owner, Martin Dell,
remembered, "we had to give
them another sandwich."

I'll have what she's having.

Estelle Reiner (as a Katz's Deli customer), in *When Harry Met Sally...*

NEW YORK LANDMARKS
1986–1995

SIX DEGREES OF SEPARATION (1993) At the METROPOLITAN MUSEUM OF ART'S ROCKEFELLER WING, designed by the architects Kevin Roche and John Dinkeloo and opened in 1981, a starkly modern structure encloses an array of ancient artifacts from Africa, Oceania and South America. Like the Temple of Dendur, its counterpart on the opposite side of the museum, the immense, glass-walled room has become a popular venue for elite cultural events—such as the black-tie reception attended in the film by the art dealer Flan Kittredge (Donald Sutherland) and his wife Ouisa (Stockard Channing).

This is rare: we got on the floor of the Stock Exchange for forty-five minutes– during trading hours. This is the real thing; there are no extras. These are real traders. Man, it was great.

Oliver Stone, writer/director, *Wall Street*

WALL STREET (1987) **By contrast, at the** NEW YORK STOCK EXCHANGE**, designed by the architect George B. Post and opened in 1903, an imposing neoclassical structure encloses an array of modern display and information systems. At several junctures, Oliver Stone's film tracks an unfolding financial manipulation right to the heart of Wall Street: the trading floor of the Exchange, which comes to life each weekday in a bedlam of frantic transactions.**

RIGHT **THE FISHER KING (1991)** To give substance to the romantic fantasies of Perry, a deranged homeless man played by Robin Williams, the filmmakers transformed the Main Concourse of GRAND CENTRAL TERMINAL into the world's largest ballroom, in which thousands of ordinary New Yorkers—policemen and firemen, rabbis and priests, businessmen and nurses—come together for a spectacular (if fleeting) waltz under the great vaulted ceiling.

ABOVE **SINGLE WHITE FEMALE (1992)** Though built as an elevator building in 1903, the 17-story ANSONIA HOTEL features an ornate open stairwell running its entire height—the ideal Gothic setting for a tense, climactic scene in which Allie (Bridget Fonda) is pursued through the building by her deranged, homicidal roommate, played by Jennifer Jason Leigh.

BROOKLYN

OPPOSITE **THE LANDLORD**
**(1970) The first location-shot
film to deal with the then-new
trend of urban homesteading
or gentrification, *The Landlord*
follows the story of a wealthy
but naive suburbanite
(Beau Bridges) who buys
a rowhouse in Park Slope,
Brooklyn—a slum district at
the time—with the intention
of evicting its black tenants
to make a private home of
his own. The film was shot
almost entirely on location
at 51 Prospect Place, off Sixth
Avenue, a block which, like
the entire district—and indeed
most of 19th century brown-
stone Brooklyn—has since
been transformed into
a desirable, increasingly
expensive destination for the
city's upper-middle classes.**

Lee Grant, playing Bridges'
suburban mother in *The
Landlord*, warily approaches
the building and its tenants.
In the background the film's
cinematographer, Gordon
Willis (wearing a dark shirt
and a framing lens attached
to a neck chain), follows
the action.

I like shooting on location. I like being inspired by a real place. Shooting in a neighborhood like [Bedford-Stuyvesant], you're influenced by the feel of the neighborhood, you're influenced by the people, you're influenced by the geography, you're influenced by seeing how the real light falls on the situation.

Ernest Dickerson, cinematographer,
Do the Right Thing

WYNN THOMAS, PRODUCTION DESIGNER, *DO THE RIGHT THING* When you do a movie like *Do the Right Thing*, so much of that intangible atmosphere you get from the location; you wouldn't get those same air molecules in a studio. There's something about being out on the streets of New York, being in Bed-Stuy, being in that actual neighborhood, that actually translates onto film in a concrete yet abstract way.

I think I would have been crucified to do a film about Bed-Stuyvesant and not shoot it in Bed-Stuy. I mean there is something about reality that you can't mess with.

Spike Lee, writer/director, *Do The Right Thing*

THIS AND OPPOSITE PAGE DO THE RIGHT THING (1989) Filmed over the summer of 1988 in the heart of Bedford-Stuyvesant—Stuyvesant Street between Quincy and Lexington Avenues—Spike Lee's film discovered a microcosm of the larger city in the well-defined vessel of a single block (OPPOSITE, TOP). Even while working its way toward a devastating climax, the film lingers on the details of daily life in a poor but vital Brooklyn neighborhood—from a stray moment of tenderness between two neighbors, played by Ruby Dee and Ossie Davis (OPPOSITE, MIDDLE), to a tense standoff between longtime residents (led by Giancarlo Esposito) and a white, upper-class newcomer played by John Savage (OPPOSITE, BOTTOM).

SMOKE (1995) **Based on a short story by Paul Auster,** *Smoke* **was set almost entirely in a smoke shop (actually a former post office space and commercial space, rented by the filmmakers) at the corner of Prospect Park West and 16th Street in Windsor Terrace (just a block or so from the setting of *Dog Day Afternoon*). In a small but meaningful ritual he has pursued every day for nearly fourteen years,** **each morning at eight a.m., just before opening his store, the shopowner Auggie Wren (Harvey Keitel) carries his camera across the street to snap a picture of what he likes to call his "little corner of the world"—a poetic evocation of the subtle (but invaluable) sense of ownership that shop proprietors in places like Brooklyn extend to the territory just outside their door.**

PAUL AUSTER We wrapped [*Blue in the Face*] on Halloween. By the time we were ready to leave the set, it was dark outside, and the Brooklyn streets were filled with children dressed in costumes. Some of them, mistaking the Brooklyn Cigar Company for an actual store, wandered in to ask for candy. The store itself might have been make-believe, but it had real candy, and so we filled the kids' trick-or-treat bags with chewing gum and chocolate bars from the shelves. It seemed like a fitting way to say good-bye to our imaginary world.

THIS PAGE **BLUE IN THE FACE** (1995) As the shooting of *Smoke* progressed in the summer of 1995, Auster and the director Wayne Wang conceived the idea for a second, quasi-improvised film that could utilize the same location and crew. Extending the lease and asking the cast and crew to stay for an extra week, the two men filmed a series of extended vignettes, interwoven with a documentary-like celebration of contemporary Brooklyn (TOP, MIDDLE AND BOTTOM).

It's a hymn to the great People's Republic of Brooklyn.
Paul Auster, writer/co-director, *Blue in the Face*

CLOCKERS (1995) In bringing Richard Price's novel to the screen, Spike Lee transferred its setting from Newark to the high-rise Gowanus Houses in Boerum Hill, Brooklyn (renamed "Nelson Mandela Houses" in the film). Making extensive use of the project's open spaces for scenes such as this confrontation between a mother and her son (Regina Taylor and Pee Wee Love) and a hostile drug dealer (Mekhi Phifer), Lee's film rendered the fraying utopian landscape of postwar public housing more fully than anyone before or since.

SOPHIE'S CHOICE (1982)
Like the celebrated William Styron novel upon which it was based, the film was largely set in "the Pink Palace"—a brightly painted Victorian rooming house in the leafy blocks just south of Prospect Park. In this scene, set in 1947, the film's main characters—Stingo (Peter MacNicol), Sophie (Meryl Streep), and Nathan (Kevin Kline)—relax atop the porch of the house used for the film, a Queen Anne-style structure at 101 Rugby Road that was painted a vivid shade of pink for the shoot— to match the description in Styron's book—then returned afterward to a subdued dove gray with modest white trim.

FANTASTIC CITY

OPPOSITE PAGE GODZILLA (1998) The introduction of computer graphics imagery ("CGI") dramatically enhanced the ability to mix action shot in the city with studio-created effects. For *Godzilla*, filmmakers combined three nights of location shooting around Madison Square—including such elements as full-sized army tanks and truckfuls of dead fish—with computer-generated images of the creature and the fleet of helicopters sent out to attack it. Despite the difficulties of shooting on location on this scale, the filmmakers were insistent. "New York has a very specific look and a very specific energy that you really can't duplicate from some other location," observed one of the film's producers, William Fay.

JOE MEDJUCK, CO-PRODUCER, *GHOSTBUSTERS* We were all living at the Mayflower Hotel just down the street, and people would come out and say, what are they doing here? They're wrecking the city—who are these people? And I'd say, this is Coppola, he's making *The Cotton Club*.

BELOW AND OVERLEAF GHOSTBUSTERS (1984) Pioneering the art of combining location action and special effects, the filmmakers shot a scene in Columbus Circle in which hundreds of extras "flee" an unseen terror coming up Broadway, then added (by way of a matte) the source of the panic: the Stay-Puft Man, a marauding one-hundred-and-twelve-foot tall marshmallow man (who actually consisted of a stunt man inside a suit).

That was so real, it was scary. For the Brooklyn Bridge shot I was far enough away so that it wasn't frightening, it was "a movie." But for the shot in Greenpoint, Brooklyn, I was somewhere along the side—close. That's the one that sent shivers down my spine—because it was troops marching through an American city, and it really got to you. They did a shot on a sidestreet that was residential, and I looked over across the street, and saw a kid open the blinds and look out, and his eyes widened in terror. And by the time I realized I should have been shooting, he was gone.

ABOVE THE SIEGE (1998) The increasing ambition of film-makers working on location in the city has been enabled, in no small part, by the ability of the Mayor's Office of Film, Theatre and Broadcasting to secure the most unlikely locations. For *The Siege*, the Mayor's Office arranged to have the Brooklyn Bridge kept clear of traffic for three hours on a Sunday morning so that a battalion of tanks and troops could be filmed crossing the span into the crowded streets of Green-point, Brooklyn—which were also cleared (on another day) to allow shooting.

OPPOSITE PAGE VANILLA SKY (2001) For the film's open-ing scene—an eerie dream sequence in which Tom Cruise finds himself in a completely deserted Times Square—the Mayor's Office arranged with the Police Department to have fifty traffic enforce-ment agents keep all vehicles and pedestrians out of the square for nearly two hours on a Sunday morning in November 2000.

LIEUTENANT JOHN BATTISTA, FORMER COMMANDING OFFICER, NYPD MOVIE-TV UNIT The producers said well, we have some requests and we don't want you to think we're crazy. We'd like to film in Times Square for about six hours—with no people, and no cars. I thought it was a joke. I said sure, now what's the real request? And they said no, we really need to do this. The following weekend I parked my unmarked car and I sat in Times Square for most of the night. I noticed that at four o'clock in the morning, all the bars emptied out, people leaving walked through Times Square, and then about 4:30 the only thing that was open was two all-night diners. And I realized that between 4:30 and 6 o'clock it was pretty much a ghost town. I mean traffic, sure, but I can always reroute traffic. And I said, okay, this might be possible. So we had a follow-up meeting and they opened the door and who comes in but Tom Cruise himself.

And he sits down and says, hello Lieutenant, I'm Tom Cruise. I need to be in Times Square with no people, no cars. And I said, Tom, let me walk you down to Times Square and let me show you what you're up against, and he said I know, but tell me what I can get. And I told him, you'll come in on Saturday night at one o'clock in the morning and you'll prep cameras and the roadway, and then once first light hits on Sunday you have to be ready to go—you'll get probably an hour, an hour and a half. And there it was, five o'clock in the morning, and there was Tom running down the middle of the street, and as you can see, every car, every *body* is gone. And it was a tremendous undertaking. It was something that to this day, people ask about, and they think it was computer generated images, but it was all live, it was all live.

THE EAST VILLAGE

MEAN STREETS (1973) One of the most influential New York location movies ever made, *Mean Streets* was actually photographed largely in Los Angeles. But the director Martin Scorsese, eager to capture the authentic feel of downtown Manhattan, arranged to spend six days shooting in New York, using a crew made up largely of NYU students, working under the guise of a thesis film. This shot, taken at the time of the film's release, shows the director at the corner of Hester and Baxter Streets, in front of the building that appears under the main titles.

While we were on the Lower East Side, a slate would come up saying *Mean Streets*, and people would get angry and say, "There's nothing wrong with these streets!" And I'd say, "No, it's only a preliminary title."

Martin Scorsese, director/co-writer, *Mean Streets*

BASQUIAT (1996) Fifteen years after he wandered the streets in *Downtown 81* (see page 125)—and eight years after his death by overdose in 1988—the artist Jean-Michel Basquiat became the subject of an entire feature film, directed by the painter Julian Schnabel. In this scene, Jeffrey Wright portrays Basquiat in his earliest days as a graffiti-artist called SAMO, pursuing his calling on an East Village wall.

Filming CHASING AMY (1997) Much of the social and cultural life of the East Village has long revolved around distinctive bars and clubs such as Meow Mix, a wittily named lesbian establishment located at the corner of Houston Street and Suffolk Street from 1994 until its closing in 2004. In this shot, Joey Lauren Adams waits outside the bar during the production of Kevin Smith's *Chasing Amy*.

SUMMER OF SAM (1999) Located for decades at 315 Bowery, the legendary club known as CBGB's (for "Country, Bluegrass, & Blues") served as an incubator for a number of musical trends, including new wave and punk rock. In a scene set in 1977 but filmed in 1999, Brooklynites Vinnie (Jon Leguizamo) and Dionna (Mira Sorvino) drive to the club to see their friend Richie (Adrien Brody) perform in a punk rock band.

SMITHEREENS (1982)

Inspired by the example of Martin Scorsese, a number of venturesome NYU film school graduates took their cameras into the streets of lower Manhattan to make their own independent features. After graduating in 1979, Susan Seidelman chose to produce and direct her first film, *Smithereens*. Working in an area she had gotten to know well as a student, Seidelman shot the low-budget film largely in the East Village, on blocks that, although now fashionable, were "at that time," Seidelman recalled, filled with "a lot of abandoned buildings and shooting galleries."

SUSAN SEIDELMAN, DIRECTOR, *SMITHEREENS* I was living in the East Village at the time, and I was noticing that there was a lot of great energy coming out of the music scene down there, and the graffiti art scene, and also there were a lot of independent filmmakers, making films for $5,000 a feature, and I thought it would be interesting to kind of tell a story about that world, of life in the East Village at that time. And I thought if I could get together a little bit of money and use the crew primarily I had worked with at NYU, that maybe I could try to do a low-budget feature.

PIECES OF APRIL (2003)

Peter Hedges' first film would extend the by now established tradition of the independent New York woman, defiantly charting her own path among the grafitti-covered (but relatively affordable) blocks of the East Village. The film follows the adventures of a rebellious daughter named April Burns (Katie Holmes) attempting, against all odds, to prepare Thanksgiving dinner for her visiting suburban family. Several wide shots capture the distinctive urban texture that, despite the growing influx of upscale shops and residents, still defines much of the area.

BACKLOT NEW YORK

Soon after the hip hangout appeared, curious natives, always on the prowl for lunch time haunts, began flocking to its doors. It was left to [the crew] on the set of *It Could Happen to You* to explain that the diner was actually a finely detailed set.

American Cinematographer, July 1994

ABOVE **CROOKLYN (1994)** Since the earliest days of Hollywood, nearly every major studio has included a permanent backlot set known as "New York Street," whose facades are actually false fronts, just inches thick. For Spike Lee's *Crooklyn*, the production designer Wynn Thomas employed the same technique on an actual "New York street"—Arlington Street in Brooklyn—to add a greater sense of spatial enclosure to what was already a well-defined urban space.

RIGHT ***batteries not included (1994)** Unable to find an actual tenement on the Lower East Side that would meet their special needs, the producers of **batteries not included* (including Steven Spielberg) asked the production designer Ted Haworth to build a new tenement building, the last surviving structure on an otherwise empty block. So convincing was Haworth's effort that city garbagemen tried to pick up the prop trash in front of the building and several people inquired about apartments for rent.

THIS PAGE **IT COULD HAPPEN TO YOU** (1994) In the summer of 1994, Tribeca residents were startled to see two historic buildings suddenly appear on an empty lot at the corner of West Broadway and North Moore Street. The two structures—which included an early 19th-century Federal-style rowhouse, its first floor converted into a 1950s modernistic coffee shop—were in fact an elaborate set created by the production designer Bill Groom, and, a few weeks later, they came down as fast as they had gone up. BELOW, RIGHT Between takes, the film's director, Andrew Bergman, jokes with Nicholas Cage (as an NYPD patrolman named Charlie Lang) and Bridget Fonda (as Yvonne Biasi, a waitress at the diner) at the counter of the coffee-shop interior, located within the exterior set and filled with convincing details, down to the attractively priced menu of specials on the wall. BOTTOM Patrolman Lang in front of the diner. RIGHT A view of the set's exterior, including a glimpse in the distance of the "Ghostbusters" firehouse (actually the functioning home of FDNY's Hook & Ladder Company #8).

ANDREW BERGMAN, DIRECTOR, *IT COULD HAPPEN TO YOU* When we shot *It Could Happen to You*, the actors preferred to sit in their chairs in the street, rather than hide in their trailers, because of the energy of the street, the everydayness of it, gave them the ease and perspective and courage to portray the very ordinary characters they had to be once the cameras rolled. Nick Cage sat in his cop's uniform and blended in so perfectly that pedestrians would stop to ask him for directions. People (tourists *and* locals) wandered into the diner we have built—lights and grip stands notwithstanding—and attempted to order lunch. We had become part of downtown life.

THE SUBWAY

SATURDAY NIGHT FEVER
(1977) Even at its low point
in the 1970s—when its aging,
poorly maintained fleet was
known around the world as a
traveling canvas for large-
scale graffiti—the subway
enjoyed a special place in the
cinematic imagination. For
Tony Manero (John Travolta),
making a difficult transition
from youth to manhood, the
train provides the crucial link
between the Brooklyn of his
past and the Manhattan that
may well hold his future.

THE WARRIORS (1979)
Based on a 1965 Sol Yurick
novel that itself drew on
the classical *Anabasis* by
Xenophon, the film trans-
forms the sprawling system
into the path of an epic
journey for a teenage gang
called the Warriors, carrying
them across the full breadth
of the five-borough city—
from the far southern end
of Brooklyn to the distant
northern edge of the Bronx,
and back—in the space of a
single arduous night.

Of all the cities in the world with subway systems, only New York has one that the whole world has ridden in its movie-fed imagination.

James Lardner, *The New York Times*, 1994

I LIKE IT LIKE THAT (1994)
For all its value as the filmic setting for dramatic, larger-than life moments, the true signifi-cance of the subway emerges in scenes such as this view

LITTLE MANHATTAN (2005)
Desperate to impress his newfound love, Rosemary (Charlie Ray), Gabe (Josh Hutcherson) agrees to travel with her from their familiar

QUEENS AND STATEN ISLAND

SPIDER-MAN (2002)

Notwithstanding its fantastic premise, the film follows the classic outlines of a "bildungsroman," the story of a boy who travels to the city, experiences adventures and heartbreak, and becomes a man. And so it begins not in the high-rise canyons of Manhattan (see page 211) but in the leafy, low-rise streets of Sunnyside, Queens, where an ordinary teenager named Peter Parker (Tobey Maguire) maintains a friendship (and well-concealed crush) on his next-door neighbor, Mary Jane (Kirsten Dunst).

ABOVE **KAL HO NAA HO (2004). As both the city and the film industry have grown more global in recent years, overseas productions have increasingly come to New York to shoot on location on the city's streets—especially the astonishingly diverse mix of communities laid out across the borough of Queens.** *Kal Ho Naa Ho* **(Tomorrow May Not Be), a Bollywood-produced romantic triangle set largely in an Indian community in Queens, features the Indian star Shah Rukh Khan, who in this scene turns the leafy streets of the** neighborhood into the setting for a spectacular dance number, set to the music of Roy Orbison's "Pretty Woman"—sung in English and Punjabi—and performed by a diverse group of passers-by, including breakdancers, punk rockers, and an African-American gospel choir. The film went on to became the fourth highest-grossing feature in the history of India.

FERRY TALES (2002). **Unlike the boroughs of Brooklyn, Queens, and the Bronx, clustered around Manhattan and laced to it by dozens of bridges, tunnels and subway lines, Staten Island sits at the far end of New York Bay, and has thus remained a world apart—a relatively sparsely settled (and, until half a century ago, largely rural) place whose primary link to the rest of the city—and primary symbol to the rest of the world—have been the big, bright-orange ferries crossing from the Battery to the slips of St. George, shown in this view from Katja Esson's 2002 film.**

NEW YORK MOMENTS
1986–1995

CROSSING DELANCEY (1988)
Izzy, a sophisticated West Sider played by Amy Irving, ventures to the Lower East Side to thank her would-be suitor Sam (Peter Riegert) for the stylish hat he has sent as gift. Her doubts about him are renewed, however, when she sees him at work among the brine-filled barrels of his father's pickle store, a setting based on—and filmed in—a local culinary landmark, Guss' Pickles, at 35 Essex Street.

OVERLEAF MO' BETTER BLUES (1990) Denzel Washington, as the gifted jazz musician Bleek Gilliam, practices his art late into the night in the solitary splendor of the walkway of the Brooklyn Bridge.

THE BASKETBALL DIARIES (1995) Based on Jim Carroll's 1978 memoir on his years as a young poet, heroin user, and basketball player (among other things), the film includes a scene of Carroll (Leonardo diCaprio) and his friends acting out the brazen and dangerous act of grabbing a free ride on the back of a city bus.

THE PROFESSIONAL (1994)
In the soft light of early morning a man quietly accompanies a 12 year-old girl (carrying his houseplant) down an empty Manhattan street—an undeniably tender scene, even if the man (Jean Reno) is actually a professional assassin who saved the life of the girl (Natalie Portman) after the murder of her parents. The two are on their way to a new hotel, where she hopes he will allow her to assist him in his unusual trade.

New York Newsday

There's More New York
In New York Newsday

THANK YOU
CALL AGAIN
NEW YORK POST

JUNGLE FEVER (1991) All across the five boroughs, for generations, candy stores and soda fountains have occupied a special place in the urban landscape. Here John Turturro mans his post in the sidewalk window of a Bensonhurst store, selling newspapers, candy bars, and lottery tickets to all who come by—and spending the hours in between simply staring out at the passing parade.

YOU'VE GOT MAIL
AS GOOD AS IT GETS
MEN IN BLACK
THE ROYAL TENENBAUMS
KISSING JESSICA STEIN
25TH HOUR
SPIDER-MAN
THE PRODUCERS
SWEET HOME ALABAMA
THE SQUID AND THE WHALE
SHAFT
CENTER STAGE
THE INTERPRETER
ALICE
MO' BETTER BLUES
HITCH
THE DEVIL'S ADVOCATE
THE BONFIRE OF THE VANITIES
GODZILLA
ONE FINE DAY
GREEN CARD
BED OF ROSES
HEIGHTS
DEATH TO SMOOCHY
13 GOING ON 30
CHELSEA WALLS
SHE'S THE ONE
THE HOURS
INSIDE MAN
MAN PUSH CART

Unimaginably, Gotham—the perennially reliable crime capital of celluloid classics from *The Naked City* to *Serpico*—is now statistically a safer city than Boise, Idaho.
The New York Times, March 1998

SIDNEY LUMET, DIRECTOR, 1998 | I just don't feel New York is menacing now. The movies and TV created a stereotype of the city—but that was then, and this is now. You have to portray New York accurately, and I'm portraying it as a beautiful city now. There is no doubt the city has changed, and the city itself is not a threat.

1996–2006

I've probably always had a very romanticized view of New York, and now, finally, the reality of New York has caught up with it.

Nora Ephron, writer/director, *You've Got Mail*

NORA EPHRON This is one of the many things in New York that not even New Yorkers know about: the beautiful flower garden at 91st Street and Riverside, which I used to walk past in the morning and think, "someday I'm going to put this in a movie."

YOU'VE GOT MAIL (1997)
As a backdrop to the unfolding relationship of Upper West Siders Joe Fox (Tom Hanks) and Kathleen Kelly (Meg Ryan)—actually *two* relationships, a tender romance online and a fierce rivalry in person—the director Nora Ephron presented a city dramatically transformed by a drop in crime and disorder to levels not seen in thirty years or more. When the couple at last come together at the end of the film, the setting is the 91st Street Community Garden in Riverside Park—an idyllic, dreamlike setting which the filmmakers used almost as is.

AS GOOD AS IT GETS (1997)
Following his daily ritual, an obsessive-compulsive writer named Melvin Udall (Jack Nicholson) walks down Sixth Avenue from his apartment to a nearby coffee shop, tracing a precisely determined path and strenuously avoiding any cracks in the sidewalk— or anything else that might trigger his anxiety.

BARRY SONNENFELD, DIRECTOR, *MEN IN BLACK* We were going to go shoot this at [Avery Fisher] Hall, and at the last minute they wanted too much money, and we came up with the Guggenheim—which was even better, because it looks like a flying saucer.

MEN IN BLACK (1997)

A spirited chase through nighttime Manhattan comes to an eye-popping climax when the alien suspect leaps up the side of the Guggenheim Museum. As has become increasingly common in recent years, the filmmakers employed computer graphics to enhance the actual location shoot at Frank Lloyd Wright's helical landmark on Fifth Avenue: the stunt man playing the alien wears a harness tied to a crane and winch by a wire—whose tell-tale line was later eliminated digitally—allowing him to seem to race up the side of the building with superhuman speed.

Filming THE ROYAL TENEN-BAUMS (2001) Having set his story in a frankly fictive New York—and specifically in a castle-like family town-house on an invented "Archer Avenue" in the Bronx—the writer and director Wes

Anderson was thrilled to locate an actual house in upper Manhattan that per-fectly suited his vision—and one, furthermore, whose interiors could be rented for six months from its new owners, who were preparing

to renovate. The distinctive turreted red-brick house, built in 1890 by the architect Adolph Hoak at the corner of Convent Avenue and 144th Street is now part of the Ham-ilton Heights Historic District.

WES ANDERSON, DIRECTOR/CO-WRITER, *THE ROYAL TENENBAUMS*

The visual idea of the movie…is that it's a kind of imaginary New York…a historical New York…combining things from a lot of different periods. Things that I'm just interested in about New York, kind of a New York literary world. It's set in the present, and it's set in New York, but…all the street names are changed, and there's a lot of anachronism…in a way that creates a slightly different world.

25TH HOUR (2002) **Near the start of the film, we see Marty Brogan (Edward Norton) sitting on a bench in Carl Schurz Park, overlooking the East River, his only company a stray dog he rescued the night before. Imaginatively taking advantage of the location—especially its distinctive metal sea rail— the director Spike Lee not only establishes the film's dark, deliberate mood but quietly hints at the story to come: a man's last day of freedom, before heading off for a long prison sentence.**

THE PRODUCERS (2005)
For the film version of Mel Brooks' musical adaptation of his own 1968 film, Lincoln Center's plaza (see page 56) was replaced with Bethesda Fountain in Central Park (the Lincoln Center fountain, built in the mid-1960s, was considered too modern for the new film, set in a mythical 1950s New York). Once again, however, the fountain's lights and waters explode magically at the decision by the mild-mannered accountant Leo Bloom (played by Matthew Broderick) to cast his lot with the ebullient—if shady—theatrical producer, Max Bialystock (Nathan Lane).

KISSING JESSICA STEIN (2001)
Desperate to escape a first date she has experimentally arranged with another woman, Jessica Stein (Jennifer Westfeldt, at right) races out into the street outside an Indian bar on East 6th Street, so nervous she drops her purse on the street. As Helen (Heather Juergensen) helps her collect her things, their relationship actually begins. (Note the colored marks on the pavement, ensuring the actors will be in the correct location for camera focus and composition.)

JENNIFER WESTFELDT, CO-WRITER AND ACTOR, *KISSING JESSICA STEIN* This is the scene where Jessica is fleeing her first date with Helen, trying desperately to hail a cab, then drops her purse all over the street. We shot it on the fly, after losing a big location at the last minute—an art gallery—that was going to take a full day. We were a tiny indie film, and we only had a permit for this one city block on the Upper East Side, so we had to scramble to find something to shoot. It was rush hour and I remember—it was hilarious—that it was truly very hard to get a cab! Then when a cab would actually stop, we would have to shoo them away—"no, no, we're acting!" I also remember almost getting hit by oncoming cars several times, and at one point a policeman came over and told us we had to be careful. Of course, we were so excited that we were capturing real city street life, I think we nodded and smiled, then tried to get close to the cars again on the next take....It was all very New York; you capture these incredible, unplanned moments on film and people think you must have scripted it.

LEFT AND BELOW SPIDER-MAN (2002) **Having gained special powers and taken on his heroic persona and costume, the film's title character leaves behind the comfortable streets of Queens (see 194) for an environment—midtown Manhattan—whose high-rise setting gives his abilities full rein. Here he confronts the paradoxes and complexities of big-city life, finding himself challenged not only by villains but by the professional life-savers—police and firemen—whose responsibilities he has taken upon himself.**

NEW YORK LANDMARKS
1996–2006

ANDY TENNANT, DIRECTOR, *SWEET HOME ALABAMA* The sequence in Tiffany's was really one for the record books. We…needed the proposal to be something special. My wife told me a story about how she had been proposed to in Tiffany's. Fortunately for me, she had said no. But I did feel like that was quite a great place, and I hadn't really seen Tiffany's [onscreen] since Audrey Hepburn had been there. So it felt to me like that could be something, and that a proposal in Tiffany's after-hours was the ticket. So [there] we are, at the real store, with the real jewelry, and the real store employees, and armed guards. Those very big shots of the store were very difficult to achieve because there wasn't anywhere to hide, so most of the crew had to be outside.

SWEET HOME ALABAMA (2002) In the film Patrick Dempsey plays Andrew Hennings, the son of the Mayor of New York and the city's most eligible bachelor—a status he at once impressively confirms and brings to an end by whisking Melanie Carmichael (Reese Witherspoon) through a darkened space that turns out to be the main floor of TIFFANY'S—where he kneels down and proposes.

The Museum of Natural History in Manhattan had had a lot of meaning to me as a kid, and it was a place that I would frequently visit with my mother. The "Squid and the Whale" diorama in the Ocean Hall was something that I was always really scared of, but…scared in that way that you like to be scared. I would try and get closer and closer to it but always…either put my hands over my face, or sort of walk very slowly and keep my distance. So that was something that I gave Walt in the movie.

ABOVE **THE SQUID AND THE WHALE** (2005) **Since at least** *The Catcher in the Rye*—in which Holden Caulfield ruminates on the unchanging American Indian dioramas that remain eternally on display—the exhibits at the **AMERICAN MUSEUM OF NATURAL HISTORY have haunted the imagination** of New York children. In Noah Baumbach's semi-autobiographical film, a diorama in the museum's Hall of Ocean Life—showing the life-and-death struggle between a sperm whale and giant squid—offers young Walt Berkman (Jesse Eisenberg) with a potent if unexpected metaphor for his conflicted family life in Brooklyn. In this view, Berkman looks out upon the centerpiece of the Hall: a suspended recreation of a blue whale—at 94 feet and 10½ tons the largest of its kind in the world.

SHAFT (2000) Little noticed by New Yorkers, the pair of neoclassical courthouses fronting the east side of FOLEY SQUARE, are among the city's most durable and familiar settings for films and TV shows, whose stories of crime and punishment often come to a denouement on the broad steps and imposing facades of the two structures. In this view from the remake of the original 1971 film (see page 106), Samuel L. Jackson, playing the detective John Shaft, stands his ground between the columns of the New York County Courthouse (designed by Guy Lowell and completed in 1927, on the left) and the U.S. Courthouse (designed by Cass Gilbert and his son, Cass Gilbert, Jr., and completed in 1936, on the right).

As a director, I come to the movies from the theater—I was a theater director for many years—and the excitement of walking onto the empty stage of a great theater for the first time never leaves you. [It was] something I wanted to convey…these kids coming onto this huge stage, the stage of the New York State Theater. There cannot be a young American ballet dancer who does not dream of stepping onto that stage.

Nicholas Hytner, director, *Center Stage*

CENTER STAGE (2001) Set in a fictional dance academy modeled on the feeder schools of the New York City Ballet and the American Ballet Theater, the film follows a group of dancers through the professional rigors and social challenges of their year-long training. In a scene early in the film, the new students sneak onto the stage of the NEW YORK STATE THEATER—the 1964 Philip Johnson and Richard Foster structure that is home to the New York City Ballet—and giddily play out their fantasies (TOP). By the film's end, with the triumphant conclusion of their first public performance, those fantasies become real (BOTTOM).

THE INTERPRETER (2004)

In an historic first, the director Sydney Pollack obtained permission to shoot inside the headquarters of the UNITED NATIONS, which had allowed no feature film crew on its premises since the shooting of *The Glass Wall* in 1953, produced when the complex was still incomplete. (Alfred Hitchcock, denied access in 1959 for *North by Northwest*, had to recreate the main lobby and the Delegates' Lounge on the MGM lot in Culver City.) Pollack managed to convince the U.N. Secretary General, Kofi Annan—as well as ambassadors from the fifteen member states of the Security Council—by offering to work only on weekends, to cover the cost of the build-ing's operation on shooting days, and to provide a substantial "good will" donation to the organization. In return, Pollack's crew was allowed to film throughout the complex, including a scene between Sean Penn and Nicole Kidman in the actual Delegates' Lounge (BOTTOM), and several scenes in the General Assembly chamber itself (DIRECTLY BELOW), which was occupied for the shoot with six hundred extras wearing everything from dark business suits to resplendent native robes and headdresses. During the prolonged filming—in what some claimed was the most authentic touch of all—several extras playing diplomats fell asleep at their seats.

THE UPPER WEST SIDE

ADAM HOLENDER, CINEMATOGRAPHER, *THE PANIC IN NEEDLE PARK* We spent weeks—including the tests maybe months—and after a while we became part of the neighborhood, to the point where we knew the hookers, we knew exactly whether someone had had a successful night or not. They went by and a couple of hours later they would come back, looking for new clients, and the police-men—everybody knew each other; it was like a Kabuki play, the life unfolded. To an enormous degree we used what the area had to offer. We were shooting, for example, on Broadway—long shots of Pacino looking for narcotics that someone was supposed to have dropped off in a phone booth or a garbage can, and all we did was to augment, slightly, the existing lighting, by having permission to put some lighting units in the stores, not to make it glossy but to bring it to reality. There were some extras, but mostly people on the streets who were totally unaware that we were filming. Then we used the interiors of the hotels in the area, which were very shabby in those days—they aren't any longer—and took several rooms of a floor of the hotel and pre-rigged it. It was freewheeling but I think it worked for the film.

JULIET TAYLOR, CASTING DIRECTOR, *THE PANIC IN NEEDLE PARK* *The Panic in Needle Park* was full of people who weren't real actors but were talented. People who'd come in off the streets. We used some real heroin addicts. It was very gritty and exciting. And a lot of wonderful New York actors were in it—Paul Sorvino, Raul Julia. What was so great about doing things in New York was the sense of reality, the sense of seeing people you'd never seen before. It became one of the great resources of shooting a movie in New York to have a real interesting, realistic, eccentric, earthy sort of cast.

THE PANIC IN NEEDLE PARK (1971) Few neighborhoods in the city have undergone more marked change over the past years than the Upper West Side. For decades, the area's thousands of middle-class families, living in spacious (if aging) prewar apartment houses, co-existed uneasily with the occupants of dozens of single-room occupancy hotels—poor, often troubled individuals who spent much of their time in the streets and a handful of decrepit public spaces. Filmed almost entirely on location in the area, *The Panic in Needle Park* focuses on a group of young drug addicts—played by Al Pacino, Kitty Winn, Raul Julia, and other actors, as well as by several actual addicts from the area—who congregate at the traffic triangles around 72nd Street and Broadway, known as "Needle Park" for the residue of heroin syringes often found underfoot.

I tell my friends where you live, they want to know how I ended up with underprivileged grandchildren.

Margaret Reynolds' mother, in *Up the Sandbox* (1972)

OPPOSITE PAGE AND ABOVE
UP THE SANDBOX (1972)
In portraying the real and fantasy life of Margaret Reynolds (Barbra Streisand)— the wife of a Columbia professor raising two children in a cramped 111th Street apartment—the film evokes the arduous, almost defiant efforts to sustain a middle-class family life on the Upper West Side in the early 1970s—from struggles with a baby carriage on the steps of a fortress-like apartment house, to forays into a cheerless, ill-maintained playground in nearby Riverside Park.

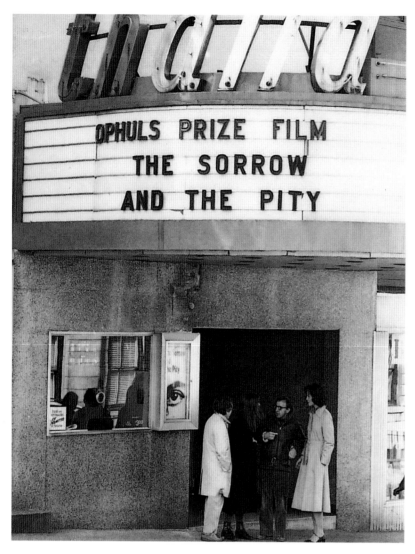

ANNIE HALL (1977) **Known for its cosmopolitan, almost Central European character— as well as its cheap rents— the Upper West Side was home in the postwar decades to many of the city's artists, writers, and musicians, along with a host of cultural landmarks, including several beloved revival houses. In an amusing scene at the end of** *Annie Hall*, **Alvy Singer (Woody Allen) and his new date (Sigourney Weaver) run into Alvy's former girlfriend, Annie Hall (Diane Keaton) outside the Thalia movie house on West 95th Street. The featured attraction is Max Ophuls' 1969 stinging documentary about French wartime collaboration,** *The Sorrow and the Pity—* **a longtime obsession of Alvy's that Annie has evidently come to share.**

THE PICK-UP ARTIST (1984) **The transformation of the Upper West Side began in earnest in the late 1970s and early 1980s, when a wave of young professionals occupied renovated tenements on Columbus Avenue and brought a new kind of street life to the area. In this view, shot on Columbus near 75th Street, Jack Jericho (Robert Downey, Jr.) sees the avenue— filled now with upscale shops and cafes—as a kind of outdoor stage for his romantic adventures and sexual overtures.**

Broadway and 72nd Street used to be called Needle Park, but now—in our new, upscale, fabulous Giuliani-ruled New York—it's called Verdi Square.

Nora Ephron, director/co-writer,
You've Got Mail

NORA EPHRON Here is a little street fair, that we built, but which goes on in New York all the time, where schools will have money-raising street fairs. It's the sort of thing that I thought was important to sell this little small-town notion—see, this is what it's really like in Manhattan, it's a neighborhood.

TOP AND BOTTOM **YOU'VE GOT MAIL** (1997) **During the mid-1990s—as the last of the tenements and single-room occupancy hotels were renovated and their former tenants displaced—the dramatic city-wide drop in crime and disorder completed the Upper West Side's metamorphosis into one of the most secure and family-friendly districts in the city—an identity celebrated in the film *You've Got Mail* by the writer/director Nora Ephron, who drew attention to the area's village-like texture of local shops, school-sponsored street fairs, and community gardens (TOP AND PAGE 206), and returned audiences to the same intersection which a quarter-century before had been the setting for *The Panic in Needle Park*, but which now, clean and refurbished, had reclaimed its forgotten original name, Verdi Square (BOTTOM).**

THE STATE OF THE ART
LOCATION SHOOTING SINCE THE 1990s

Filming ALICE (1990) Thanks to a steady stream of technical and logistical advances, by the 1990s location shooting in New York had lost much of the improvised, hit-or-miss quality of earlier years and instead had become nearly as routinized as working on a stage. In this view of Woody Allen's 1990 feature, a crew films Mia Farrow and Joe Mantegna in a basic "walk-and-talk" shot as they amble down East 95th Street, deep in conversation. To capture their movement, a 35mm Panaflex camera has been fitted onto a "dolly sled"— a rolling platform large enough to hold the operator and his assistant, carefully pulled along a length of track by a grip who watches the actors and perfectly matches their pace. Adjacent to the camera is a 12,000-watt metal-halide lamp, whose light output, softened by a silk diffuser, will subtly "punch out" the faces of the actors against the background. Supervising the setup is the director of photography, Carlo di Palma, wearing a long coat and tracing the path of the camera.

Filming MO' BETTER BLUES (1990) This moody shot of Bill Nunn and Jeff Watts was filmed by director Spike Lee in a lower Manhattan alleyway—one of the handful of mid-block thoroughfares downtown that have long been favored among filmmakers for their narrow confines and photogenic mix of textures and shadows—especially when dramatically backlit, as in this set-up.

Filming HITCH (2004) Among the advances that took the guesswork out of location shooting was video assist, first used commonly for commercials in the 1970s and soon after adapted for features. Today virtually every shoot includes a "video village," a cluster of monitors through which the director and cinematographer—neither of whom typically looks through the viewfinder during filming—can follow and play back each shot. "It lets the filmmakers check movement, composition, dialogue," the veteran camera operator Sol Negrin has observed, and "allows for the director to be satisfied with the choreography of the shot." Here the actress Eva Mendes reviews her performance at the corner of Greene and Spring Streets in SoHo.

Filming THE DEVIL'S ADVOCATE (1997) By 2000, advances in cameras, rigs, lenses, lighting, and film stock had combined to dramatically streamline the process of location shooting. A crucial advance for location work was the Steadicam, a stabilizing rig invented by the cinematographer Garrett Brown, which allows an operator to walk forward or backward while carrying a movie camera, without any visible jiggling or shaking in the frame— and thus plunge unfettered into the street life of the city. In this view, Al Pacino and Keanu Reeves, striding through the streets of Chinatown, are filmed by an operator holding a 35mm portable Panavision camera—a battery-powered, sound-synchronized, noiseless device weighing just fifty pounds—on a Steadicam rig. By contrast, see page 94 for a typical location setup in the 1960s, requiring nearly a quarter-ton of unwieldy, difficult-to-maneuver equipment.

THE BONFIRE OF THE VANITIES (1990) As location shooting grew more common, filmmakers routinely called for more elaborate set-ups, undaunted by logistical challenges. For Brian de Palma's adaptation of Tom Wolfe's novel, filmmakers took over a full-block stretch of Park Avenue and 74th Street for a day and night, in order to film a scene of Sherman McCoy (Tom Hanks) leaving his apartment house, amidst a thunderstorm, to walk his dog—and call his mistress. Work on the shoot, which began at 8 a.m., included the installation of a prop phone booth, the placement of two cranes—each over a hundred feet tall—to hold the rain sprinklers that would drench the sidewalk, and the location of generators to power the lights and wind machines that would simulate the storm. The shoot itself did not begin until 11:20 p.m., required ten takes, and ended at 1 a.m.

It was truly an enormous mustering of manpower and trucks. Usually you can just light a single story— after all, your actors aren't any taller than that—but we had to light twenty stories for our star. And since [the director Roland Emmerich] was panning the camera around, we were lighting up twenty stories for blocks and blocks in all directions. There was a *Godzilla* traffic report each morning, warning commuters where we'd be shooting each day.

Dean Devlin, producer, *Godzilla*

Filming GODZILLA (1998) To shoot the backgrounds for a crucial confrontation around Madison Square (see page 180 for completed effect), the producers created one of the largest film locations ever seen in Manhattan, closing several blocks of Broadway and 23rd Street for several nights, and floodlighting dozens of skyscrapers to a height of two hundred feet or more.

ROOFTOPS

LEFT GREEN CARD (1990) For Brontë (Andie MacDowell)—a young New York woman feigning marriage to an illegal French alien, Georges (Gerard Depardieu), in order to qualify for a garden-filled penthouse on West 76th Street—the building's rooftop proves an ideal stage on which to enact the scenes that will make up a convincing photo album of their imaginary multi-year relationship, from beach holidays to ski vacations.

RIGHT BED OF ROSES (1996) Time and again, filmmakers have employed the rooftops of New York as settings for romance—finding in them surprisingly intimate places, from which the city lays itself out, as if for the pleasure of the lovers who overlook it. In this view, Christian Slater, as a Wall Street financier who has left his job to become a florist, surprises Mary Stuart Masterson with a rustic picnic on a landscaped rooftop, high above the streets of Chelsea.

HEIGHTS (2005) Not even
the utilitarian character of
most city rooftops—such as
that of the Municipal Building
in lower Manhattan, in this
view—seems to preclude them
as their use as a setting for the
most intimate conversations,
in this case between Elizabeth
Banks and Matt Davis.

THE DEVIL'S ADVOCATE (1997) The terror of falling from a high rooftop, played out in numbers of action movies and thrillers, remains implicit (but perhaps for that reason all the more effective) in this scene of an arrogantly charming but shadowy law partner (Al Pacino) inter- viewing an ambitious new associate (Keanu Reeves) on a rooftop terrace outside his downtown Manhattan office— one whose unusual design (created through a combina- tion of location shooting and computer graphics) includes a broad reflecting pool but no safety railing whatsoever (TOP). This shot reveals how the scene's vertiginous effect was created using a platform raised several feet off a wide roof—and located nowhere near its edge (BOTTOM).

TIMES
SQUARE

Photograph courtesy of Museum of the Moving Image / Munkacsi Collection.

OPPOSITE PAGE AND RIGHT

MIDNIGHT COWBOY (1969)

While virtually every corner of the city has witnessed dramatic shifts in recent decades, it is the transformation of Times Square that has come to stand for the changes in New York itself—in part because that transformation has been especially dramatic, in part because of the area's crucial place in the American imagination, but also in part because those changes have been documented so thoroughly—and powerfully—by filmmakers drawn to the visual dazzle and human complexities of the area. Rarely, for example, has any urban district, anywhere, been rendered more hauntingly or poignantly than late-1960s Times Square in *Midnight Cowboy*, as director John Schlesinger and cinematographer Adam Holender, both new to New York, follow an even newer arrival—a naive would-be hustler from Texas, played by Jon Voight—as he exhausts his meager resources and is forced to meander the brightly lit but unforgiving streets, homeless, penniless, and miserable.

ADAM HOLENDER, CINEMATOGRAPHER, *MIDNIGHT COWBOY* Times Square was a difficult location from the logistics point of view—in order to capture the reality of it. I had this idea how to shoot day scenes: we created a Trojan horse. We built an oversized wooden telephone booth, we mounted the camera and the tripod inside, we put a camera operator and a focus-puller inside, with enough [film] magazines to last a long while. That whole box was unloaded on 42nd Street, on the sidewalk, and therefore we were able to slide the wooden door open and shoot people who were on the street. Everything worked very nicely, but Schlesinger was always excited and kept running back and forth to this box, knocking on it saying, did you get this, did you get that? After a while, people caught on. For night shots, the camera supplier Dick DiBona equipped us with very fast lenses—actually they were made for military use—and they worked very well. We used handheld cameras, we used black-and-white film, color film, we pushed it, we did things that were unacceptable for a studio film.

It's all great that this is on [film] because Times Square looks like Disneyland now, and this is for posterity. This is the *real* Times Square.

Robin Johnson, actor, *Times Square*

ALAN MOYLE, DIRECTOR, *TIMES SQUARE* (1980) We closed off Times Square and it was a big deal at the time, and of course we couldn't afford the number of actors to actually fill the street. We had one night to do all this.

TIMES SQUARE (1980)
Propelled by a punk rock soundtrack that includes Lou Reed, Patti Smith, and the Ramones, the film follows the adventures of two runaway girls (Robin Johnson and Trini Alvarado) who, calling themselves "the Sleeze Sisters," engage in a series of antics around Times Square—climaxing with this guerilla concert atop the marquee of the Times Square Theater on West 42nd Street, at the time a "grind house" playing cheap action films. Despite its claims of gritty authenticity, the film offers a "pastoral vision," argues the urbanist Marshall Berman, "that portrays [West 42nd Street] as a magic kingdom where adolescents are protected from all the pressures that haunt every American high school. It's the first 42nd Street theme park."

TOOTSIE (1982) The actual transformation of Times Square began on the area's periphery, where a group of small commercial buildings along 42nd Street between Ninth and Tenth Avenues was transformed in the early 1980s into a series of off-Broadway playhouses called Theater Row. The urbane, pedestrian-friendly streetscape soon became the setting for *Tootsie*, featuring Dustin Hoffman and Jessica Lange as soap-opera stars who work from the adjacent National Video Center, at the Tenth Avenue end of the block.

DEATH TO SMOOCHY (2002)
Shot in the heart of Times Square, looking north from 43rd Street, this romantic moment between Edward Norton and Catherine Keener not only captures the stunning visual resurgence of the area—whose famed lights and signs had grown larger, brighter, and more technically sophisticated than ever before—but hints at the underlying economic transformation of the district, which by the start of the 21st century was not only a center of popular culture but corporate home to many of the biggest entertainment companies and media conglomerates in the world. In this scene, Keener plays a cynical production executive who at last gives in romantically to Norton, a sweet-hearted children's television performer.

13 GOING ON 30 (2004) The vision of Times Square as a dazzling but safe playground for adolescents—a fantasy at the time of 1980's *Times Square*—had become commonplace by the start of the 21st century, especially onscreen. In this scene, Jenna Rink (Jennifer Garner)— a 13 year-old girl somehow transformed into the body and life of a thirty-year-old New York career-woman—revels in the brilliant lights and signs of the Square from the open top of a limousine.

THE ART OF THE STILL PHOTOGRAPHER

MIDNIGHT COWBOY (1969)
Virtually since the birth of the movies, still photographers have been an integral part of the production process. Frame enlargements from actual 35mm film footage are generally not a suitable source for publicity stills or big "one-sheet" posters, and in any case can not capture the "behind the scenes" views that are so often part of the marketing of a feature film. But the abiding value of still photographers is more than

a technical matter. At their best, still photographers can capture images that, without benefit of movement or dialogue, manage to bring alive—and instantly communicate—the narrative or thematic essence of a two-hour feature film. Among the greatest still photographers in film history was the Hungarian-born Muky Munkácsi, who emigrated to America in 1936 to work at Warner Bros. and became known in the postwar years for his distinctive stills,

images comparable in quality to almost any photographic work being done at the time. (His brother Martin Munkácsi, also an emigre, became a celebrated photojournalist and fashion photographer.) This view of "Ratso" Rizzo (Dustin Hoffman) and Joe Buck (Jon Voight) takes place at the boarded-up entrance to an abandoned West Village building in which the two indigents find rudimentary shelter. (Other images by Muky can be found on 96, 234, and 235.)

UP THE DOWN STAIRCASE (1967) Taken by an unidentified studio photographer, this view of Sylvia Barrett (Sandy Dennis), a first-year public high-school teacher making her way through the unfriendly streets of East Harlem, inevitably evokes one of the classic images of urban tension, "American Girl in Italy," the 1951 photograph by Ruth Orkin of a single young woman, surrounded by leering men, walking hurriedly through the streets of Rome.

HANNAH AND HER SISTERS (1986) Brian Hamill, a noted New York photographer who has been shooting stills for Woody Allen's films since *Annie Hall*, captured this haunting image of a despondent Mickey Sachs (Allen)— profoundly shaken by a (somewhat distant) brush with death—entering the lobby of the Metro Theater, the venerable Art Deco movie house at 100th Street and Broadway, since closed.

BRIAN HAMILL, STILL PHOTOGRAPHER, *HANNAH AND HER SISTERS* Being a still photographer is being able to get along with people in small tight rooms and spaces, and that's part of the deal with making movies in New York, you always have tight spaces, especially on location interiors. You have to be able to get the photographs, and you have to be unobtrusive in getting them—but you can't be shy about getting them, you have to get in there and capture the dramatic point of each scene in a visual still; that's what scene stills are all about. I always try to get a visual representation, a graphic if you will, of the theme or motif of the movie. But it's not just to get the scene stills; I approach every movie like a photojournalist where I'm telling a story—the making of a movie.

NEW YORK MOMENTS
1996–2006

CHELSEA WALLS (2001) In Ethan Hawke's film version of Nicole Burdette's play— a rondelet of five stories set in the venerable Chelsea Hotel on West 23rd Street— Rosario Dawson steps onto one of the narrow cast-iron balconies outside each room that are a distinctive feature of the Edwardian- era structure.

SHE'S THE ONE (1996)
Francis Fitzpatrick (Mike McGlone) and his brother Mickey (Ed Burns) find their way to a pair of familiar stools at McHale's Bar on Eighth Avenue, where they bemoan their various troubles with women.

THE HOURS (2002) **Echoing the travels of Virginia Woolf's fictional character, Clarissa Dalloway, through the streets of London, a New York woman called Clarissa Vaughan (Meryl Streep) journeys from the comfortable confines of a Greenwich Village flower shop to a bleaker precinct of the meat-packing district, there to call upon Richard Brown (Ed Harris), a writer dying of AIDS.**

ONE FINE DAY (1996) Outside the Carnegie Deli on Seventh Avenue and 55th Street (see 158), Jack Taylor (George Clooney) and young Sammy Parker (Alex D. Linz) share a manly ritual: waiting on the street as their female companions—Sammy's mother Melanie and Jack's daughter Maggie—refresh themselves inside.

MAN PUSH CART (2005)

Every morning, a Pakistani immigrant named Ahmad (played by Ahmad Ravzi), must drag his heavy push-cart through the traffic-filled streets of Manhattan, spend the day selling coffee and doughnuts to brusque, hurried New Yorkers, then drag the pushcart that evening back before retiring to a tiny apart-ment in Brooklyn, only to repeat the process the next day. Ramin Bahrani, an Iranian-American filmmaker working in New York, presents an almost Sisyphean portrait of one of the countless newcom-ers to the city who have given up their lives and home (and in Ahmad's case, a brief career as a Pakistani rock star) to eke out the barest of livings in the globalized metropolis of contemporary New York.

MAD HOT BALLROOM (2005)

The film follows the experience of three New York public schools as they take part in the American Ballroom Theater's Dancing Classrooms program, which teaches ball-room dancing to fifth-graders from sixty schools across the city, leading to an annual competition. Here four students from P.S. 115 in Washington Heights—a largely Dominican neighbor-hood at the northern tip of Manhattan—rehearse their turns atop one of the rugged outcroppings of granite that dot the area.

OFF
THE SET

Filming ROSEMARY'S BABY (1968) Despite the aura of excitement that surrounds the act of shooting on the location, the actual process inevitably involves frequent periods of inactivity, as new set-ups are prepared or technical problems addressed. Views of actors caught in those moments, usually still in wardrobe, often carry a haunting—and haunted—quality, as if the performer is somehow absent, remaining instead inside the character they are playing, back on the set itself. Here Mia Farrow, dressed as the young housewife Rosemary, waits between scenes outside the Dakota apartment house during the shooting of *Rosemary's Baby*.

MOLLY RINGWALD, ACTOR, *THE PICK-UP ARTIST* As everyone says—and it's true—the city has an energy that can't be duplicated. They can call Toronto "New York" all they want, but if it's [supposed to be] New York and it's shot in Toronto—it's like there's a character missing. The life of the party…as it were.

Filming THE PICK-UP ARTIST (1984) Waiting between takes on a scene shot in the West 70s (and later cut from the picture), the film's female lead, Molly Ringwald, wears a similar look of abstracted concentration, as she and her co-star, Robert Downey, Jr. pass the time sitting in the portable wood-and-canvas "director's chairs" that have been a presence in location shoots since the earliest days of the film industry.

Filming I SHOT ANDY WARHOL (1996) **Off-the-set images of location films that take place in historic periods, or are based on real-life figures, carry their own haunting quality. In this view, actors and crew—including the actor Jared Harris, playing Andy Warhol—prepare for a scene set outside Warhol's "Factory" on Union Square West (though actually filmed on West 20th Street between Fifth and Sixth Avenues).**

MARY HARRON, DIRECTOR, *I SHOT ANDY WARHOL* The photo with Jared Harris is somewhere in Chelsea. We were waiting to shoot the scene in the new Factory, where Valerie shoots Warhol. We could only shoot a narrow piece of the block, because we couldn't dress anything, so we just had to choose a small section that looked "sixties."

Filming INSIDE MAN (2006) **Among the empty nighttime canyons of lower Manhattan's financial district, the director Spike Lee and his longtime leading man, Denzel Washington, enjoy a laugh between shots while resting on a camera platform that is set up to dolly almost the entire length of William Street toward Wall Street in the distance.**

ETERNAL SUNSHINE OF THE SPOTLESS MIND (2004) **The actor Jim Carrey, in wardrobe as the film's leading character Joel Barish, stands on the middle of Orchard Street on the Lower East Side, while crew members prepare for the next set-up.**

THE HONEYMOONERS
NAKED CITY
MCCLOUD
CAGNEY & LACEY
KOJAK
LAW & ORDER
COMMERCIAL FOR NIKE
COMMERCIAL FOR 2001 TONY AWARDS AND VISA
"LOVE IS STRONG" MUSIC VIDEO
"THE LATE SHOW" WITH DAVID LETTERMAN
SESAME STREET
SEX AND THE CITY
THE SOPRANOS

1966-

TV

2006

BEFORE THE MAYOR'S OFFICE

OPPOSITE **Publicity still for "THE HONEYMOONERS"**
Like motion pictures, the television industry had its earliest origins not in Los Angeles but in New York. Emerging in the late 1940s and early 1950s as an outgrowth of network radio—whose studios had always been located primarily in Manhattan—the infant medium revolved around New York not only as a center of production but as the setting for many of its most memorable programs, including "The Honeymooners," a half-hour comedy spun off in 1955 from a variety show hosted and produced by the Brooklyn-born performer Jackie Gleason. Set in a drab two-room apartment at "358 Chauncey Street" in the Bensonhurst section of Brooklyn, the series followed the misadventures of a bus driver named Ralph Kramden (played by Gleason himself), a sewer worker named Ed Norton (played by Art Carney, pictured here), and their long-suffering wives (Audrey Meadows and Joyce Randolph). Like almost all early television, the series was shot entirely on a stage set, and used actual city locations only for the occasional publicity stills such as this.

"NAKED CITY" Inspired by the landmark 1948 feature, *The Naked City*—the first sound film to be shot almost entirely on location in New York (page 34)—the television series "Naked City" broke with tradition by being filmed "in the streets and buildings of New York itself," as the show's unseen narrator reminded audiences every week. Remembered for its famous closing lines (also drawn from the feature)—"There are eight million stories in the Naked City. This has been one of them"—the series, which ran from 1958 to 1963, provided the template for a remarkably durable television staple: the location-shot New York police drama, a steady presence on network prime-time schedules ever since, from "McCloud" and "Kojak," to "Cagney & Lacey" and "The Equalizer," to "Law & Order" and its spinoffs. But more than any of its successors—except "Law & Order"—the original "Naked City" made the city itself its primary focus. As the series progressed—and especially after it expanded in 1962 to a full hour in length, allowing for more complex (and often strikingly unresolved) storylines—its narrative core shifted away from its cadre of NYPD detectives (including Detective Adam Flint, played by Paul Burke, shown here) to those they were trying to apprehend or protect; as the critic Todd Gitlin noted, "the regular cops faded into the background, while the foreground belonged to each week's new character in the grip of the city."

THE POLICE DRAMAS

"MCCLOUD" Like "Naked City," the police drama "McCloud," which ran from 1970 to 1977, drew its premise and inspiration directly from a New York feature film, *Coogan's Bluff*, whose script by Herman Miller followed the "fish-out-of-water" adventures of a Western lawman (Clint Eastwood) relentlessly pursuing an escaped convict across Manhattan (see page 95). For the TV series, Dennis Weaver played Deputy U.S. Marshal Sam McCloud, based in Taos, New Mexico who is transferred to "special assignment" in New York. Claiming he was in the city "to observe and learn," McCloud would nonetheless find himself each week in the thick of an unfolding crime investigation, in pursuit of which he more than once found it necessary to mount an NYPD patrol horse and gallop through the busy streets of the city. Though the series included a number of sequences shot on location in New York, (especially in its first few seasons), the shows were filmed primarily on the Universal Studios backlot in southern California.

"CAGNEY & LACEY"
Running from 1982 to 1988, "Cagney & Lacey" reflected the changing character of the city's police department by focusing on two women detectives, Christine Cagney (Sharon Gless, at left) and Mary Beth Lacey (Tyne Daley). The series, which utilized extensive location shooting (such as this view on a tenement rooftop), often drew its storylines—as "Law & Order" would later—from actual city incidents, such as the racially motivated killing of a young black man, Michael Griffith, in Howard Beach, Queens in December, 1986.

"KOJAK" For six years, from 1973 to 1978, the police drama "Kojak" followed the adventures of Lieutenant Theo Kojak (Telly Savalas), a bald, Greek-American detective attached to the NYPD's 13th Precinct. Though the series was promoted as being filmed on location (in publicity stills such as this view, taken on the plaza at Lincoln Center) and did in fact spend several days shooting in the city each season, "Kojak" (like "McCloud") was actually produced primarily at Universal Studios in Hollywood, relying on extensive second-unit footage of New York for establishing shots and backgrounds.

LAW & ORDER

There is no substitute for New York City— the look, the people, the locations. That is what differentiates "Law & Order" from other so-called New York shows that are actually shot in Los Angeles or other locales. It brings a certain cinema verité that you cannot replicate. The lighting, the backgrounds, the locations—New York is unlike any other city in the world, and that uniqueness shows on screen.

Dick Wolf, executive producer, "Law & Order"

"LAW & ORDER" Though the location-shot police "procedural" drama stretches back to the late 1950s, the form was all but revolutionized in 1990, when the veteran producer Dick Wolf created "Law & Order," an hour-long series whose episodes spend their first half looking at the police department's efforts to solve a crime, and their second half on the District Attorney's attempts to prosecute the suspect. After more than a decade and a half of continuous production—the longest run in history for a live-action primetime American television show—the series has become a virtual industry, spinning off two additional hour-long shows ("Law & Order: Special Victims Unit," which premiered in 1999, and "Law & Order: Criminal Intent" which began two years later), employing over a thousand New Yorkers, and spending more than a million dollars a week during production. (The Mayor's Office recently calculated that the original series alone has pumped over $750 million into the city's economy in the sixteen years it has been on the air.) Produced almost entirely in New York, the series uses location shooting more extensively than any television series before it, setting not only action sequences but many of its characters' ordinary conversations in the city's streets, parks, and public spaces, thus making New York the series' most consistent element—especially given its constantly evolving cast of characters, including detectives Mike Logan (Chris Noth) and Max Greevey (George Dzundza), shown questioning witnesses on a Manhattan sidewalk (OPPOSITE PAGE); district attorney Jack McCoy (Sam Waterston) and assistant district attorney Claire Kincaid (Jill Hennessy), confronting a suspect in Central Park (LEFT, ABOVE), and detectives Leonard R. Briscoe (Jerry Orhbach) and Reynaldo Curtis (Benjamin Bratt) taking a coffee break on Worth Street in lower Manhattan (LEFT, BELOW).

DICK WOLF Even though the city has experienced a dramatic drop in crime and disorder since 1990, we still read about victims on a daily basis. When I pitched the show to [NBC president] Brandon Tartikoff in 1988, he asked, "what is the 'bible' for the show?" I said, "the front page of the *New York Post.*"

COMMERCIALS AND MUSIC VIDEOS

COMMERCIAL FOR NIKE
Although the commercial business is no longer the near-exclusive province of New York that it once was (in the 1960s fully 85% of all American television commercials were produced in New York), the city remains a major production center for commercials and other kinds of marketing and promotional films, thanks in large part to its continuing role as the undisputed advertising capital of the country. It also remains the most popular urban setting for commercials, such as this Nike promotional film about an older runner who makes his way from borough to borough.

**COMMERCIAL FOR 2001
TONY AWARDS AND VISA**
This commercial shot entirely
in black and white, seeks to
capture and re-ignite the energy
and excitement of the city's
theatrical community through
a stylish, cross-sectional look
at some of Broadway's places,
people, and rituals.

I got more phone calls from people asking how much motion control and miniatures we used. They were very disappointed to hear that there was no motion control, and no miniatures.

Fred Raimondi, visual effects supervisor, "Love is Strong"

"LOVE IS STRONG" MUSIC VIDEO (1994) Directed by David Fincher, with special visual effects by Fred Raimondi and Digital Domain, this stunning music video places the Rolling Stones and several comely female companions—all suddenly grown to eighty or ninety feet tall—among the streets, parks, waters, rooftops, and bridges of New York City. Using a new software program called Flame, the effects team digitally combined two dozen actual New York location settings with the movement of the band members and other performers, shot on a stage using a "green screen" background. A technique called Derivative Motion Blur added realism to the sequences by suggesting a slight shake to the camera as one of the giant figures falls to the pavement, or kicks the immense stone abutment of the Williamsburgh Bridge. Giant water tanks serve as a percussion set for the drummer Charlie Watts; young women rise from Central Park Lake or the East River and shake themselves dry, another girl stretches out across an entire roof to sunbathe, and the band comes together at the end in the middle of Central Park, whose mighty trees scarcely come up to their knees.

TALK SHOWS AND CHILDREN'S PROGRAMS

"THE LATE SHOW" WITH DAVID LETTERMAN The television talk show began in New York, an outgrowth of the traditional radio talk shows, which (like their televised successors) fed on the never-ending stream of entertainers and celebrities performing in (or simply passing through) the city. David Letterman's late night show, which in 1992 established itself in the former Ed Sullivan Theater (itself the site of one of America's most popular televised variety shows in the 1950s and '60s) has distinguished itself in recent years by often leaving the confines of its stage to make imaginative use of its urban setting. On September 26th, 2002, in a light rain, the aerial artist Philippe Petit—who in August 1974 had crossed between the towers of the World Trade Center—performed a televised high-wire walk across Broadway, making his transit on a 7/8" diameter steel cable, 120 feet long, strung 160 feet above the street. When one stagehand wondered if the poor weather would force him to cancel the performance, Petit replied firmly, "There are cameras. There are people. I walk." Three weeks later, on November 11th, 2002, the evening's broadcast ended with a fireworks display by the Grucci family, who, on Letterman's go-ahead, lit two long fuses that ran down the façade of the building, setting off 1,020 individual fireworks placed atop the theater marquee.

"SESAME STREET"

Premiering in November 1969, "Sesame Street," an hour-long children's morning show and the flagship of the Children's Television Workshop (now the Sesame Workshop), quickly revolutionized the world of educational broadcasting, and has since become the most popular children's show in history, televised in more than 120 countries around the globe. In distinction from the traditionally rural or small-town settings of much children's programming, the creators of "Sesame Street" deliberately set their show on a typical city block, constructed on a stage at the Kaufman Astoria Studios in Queens, and inspired by the architecturally and socially diverse streets of New York. Over the years, the show has also taken advantage of its urban setting by venturing out of doors to locations all around the city, including Chinatown (left) and Central Park (below), where these views of Big Bird (Carroll Spinney) and his friends were taken.

THE CABLE REVOLUTION

In New York City, you walk out the door and you do not know what is going to happen. There's such potential for poetry.
Sarah Jessica Parker, actor, co-producer, "Sex and the City"

MICHAEL PATRICK KING, PRODUCER, "SEX AND THE CITY" The city is a great turbine engine for everything you write. It's a conveyor belt for characters and bachelors and people coming and going. You have the city, the four girls, and some broken hearts. Go.

"SEX AND THE CITY" Based on the best-selling novel by Candace Bushnell, the series, which ran on HBO from 1999 to 2004, marked the advent of cable television as a major force in New York location production. Freed from the restraints on subject matter and language that have traditionally limited network television, and willing to pursue more complex storylines and adult themes, episodic cable series found a natural setting in contemporary New York—above all, "Sex and the City," whose basic premise was simply the intertwining social and professional lives of four young Manhattan women (played by Sarah Jessica Parker, Cynthia Nixon, Kristin Davis and Kim Cattrall). Initially cynical about the realities of single life in the big city, the series grew increasingly romantic as it continued, presenting not only a glamorous vision of urban life, but (especially after September 11th) demonstrating a frankly emotional commitment to the city and its values.

Making more extensive use of New York locations than any other show on television (except perhaps "Law & Order") the series was set in everyday urban environments—streets, parks, stoops, apartment house entrances—as well as highly recognizable New York settings, from civic landmarks such as Columbus Circle (OVERLEAF) to fashionable nightclubs, restaurants and stores, such as Magnolia Bakery on Bleecker Street in Greenwich Village.

"THE SOPRANOS" Though set primarily in the suburbs of northern New Jersey, just across the Hudson River from New York, where its world of Mafia families make their home, the series often ventures into the city. In this dramatic evening view, family chieftain Tony Soprano (James Gandolfini) confronts his powerful New York counterpart, John "Johnny Sack" Sacramoni (Vincent Curatola), in the Empire Stores Park near the Brooklyn foot of the Brooklyn Bridge.

THE CITY INFUSES EVERY FRAME...

BY NORA EPHRON

A few years ago, I was on a panel about New York, one of the milder results of September 11, and all of us on the panel were asked to consider a wonderful question: When did you first realize you were a New Yorker? Among those on the panel were a former mayor who'd grown up in Brooklyn, an Armenian immigrant who now heads the Carnegie Foundation, an anchorwoman from Indiana, and a writer from Ireland, and we all had answers. Mine went something like this: I was born in New York, and after a few years my parents moved us to Los Angeles. And I have an absolutely clear memory of the moment I knew I was a New Yorker: I was attending my first day of school on Doheny Drive in Beverly Hills, the sun was shining: Dappled light was coming through the trees, it was an absolutely gorgeous day, I was surrounded by happy laughing children, and all I could think was, "What am I doing here?" I was five years old. And I absolutely knew—I'm not exaggerating—that I had to get back to where I belonged.

It's probably worth mentioning that the reason my parents moved to California was because they became screenwriters. In those days, if you were a screenwriter, you had to live in Los Angeles. There was no movie business outside of that city, and no real way to be part of it. My parents were part of a diaspora of displaced New Yorkers, all of them complaining ritualistically about how impossible it was to find a decent bagel in southern California. They were readers, they were political, and they were smart, smart enough to know that they'd left a piece of themselves behind when they moved out there, and I'm not talking about selling their souls or anything as mundane as that: I'm talking about the fact that people who think of themselves as New Yorkers do better in New York. They do better because there's no disconnect between who they are and where they live. They do better because they live in a place where movies are not the center of the universe. They do better because, like Betty Smith's famous ailanthus tree that grows in Brooklyn, they thrive only in this particular metropolis. California is fine, Fred Allen famously said, if you're an orange.

Those of us who live here and work in the movie business have chosen to because we can't conceive of being anywhere else—personally or artistically. We feed off the city and its life, and the city infuses every frame of the movies that are made here. A couple of years ago, I cut a montage of New York films for the Oscars, and what struck me as I went through the amazing body of work that's been shot here was that New York was much more than the location for these movies—it was a character in them, it was the context, it was the *sine qua non*. Movies made here—like *Mean Streets*, *Dog Day Afternoon*, *Carnal Knowledge*, *Desperately Seeking Susan*, *The Godfather*, and *Annie Hall*, to name a few—exist because of the city; they would never have been created but for the effect of the city on the people who wrote and directed them. Woody Allen's New York, Martin Scorsese's New York, and Spike Lee's New York have only one thing in common: New York. As F. Scott Fitzgerald wrote of the city, it always manages to "promise...all the mystery and beauty of the world."

The editors of *Scenes from the City* and the Mayor's Office of Film, Theatre and Broadcasting wish to acknowledge all of the gifted and dedicated men and women who created the images in this book, including the cinematographers, camera operators, and other crew members who shaped the film and television sequences presented in these pages. We also wish to offer a special acknowledgment of the talents and hard work of the film industry's still photographers, whose evocative and powerful images literally made this book possible.

FILMOGRAPHY

In addition to the title, release date, and original releasing studio, the following information is provided:

D director

W screenwriter (and author of original source material, in case of adaptation)

C cinematographer

12 Angry Men (1957), United Artists D Sidney Lumet W Reginald Rose, from a teleplay by Reginald Rose C Boris Kaufman

13 Going on 30 (2004), Columbia Pictures D Gary Winick W Josh Goldsmith, Cathy Yuspa C Don Burgess

15 Minutes (2001), New Line Cinema D John Herzfeld W John Herzfeld C Jean Yves Escoffier

25th Hour (2002), Buena Vista Pictures D Spike Lee W David Benioff, from a novel by David Benioff C Rodrigo Prieto

Across the Sea of Time (1995), Columbia Pictures D Stephen Low W Andrew Gellis C Andrew Kitzanuk

After Hours (1985), Warner Bros. D Martin Scorsese W Joseph Minion C Michael Ballhaus

Alice (1990), Orion Pictures D Woody Allen W Woody Allen C Carlo Di Palma

American Psycho (2000), Columbia Pictures D Mary Harron W Mary Harron, Guinevere Turner, from a novel by Bret Easton Ellis C Andrzej Sekula

Anderson Tapes, The (1971), Columbia Pictures D Sidney Lumet W Frank R. Pierson, from a novel by Lawrence Sanders C Arthur J. Ornitz

Annie Hall (1977), United Artists D Woody Allen W Woody Allen, Marshall Brickman C Gordon Willis

April Fools, The (1969), National General Pictures D Stuart Rosenberg W Hal Dresner C Michel Hugo

As Good as It Gets (1997), Columbia Pictures D James L. Brooks W James L. Brooks, Mark Andrus C John Bailey

Barefoot in the Park (1967), Paramount Pictures D Gene Saks W Neil Simon, from a play by Neil Simon C Joseph LaShelle

Basketball Diaries, The (1995), New Line Cinema D Scott Kalvert W Bryan Goluboff, from a memoir by Jim Carroll C David Phillips

Basquiat (1996), Miramax Films D Julian Schnabel W John Bowe, Julian Schnabel, Lech J. Majewski, Michael Thomas Holman C Ron Fortunato

*batteries not included (1987), Universal Pictures D Matthew Robbins W Matthew Robbins, Mick Garris, Brad Bird, Brent Maddock, S.S. Wilson C John McPherson

Bed of Roses (1996), New Line Cinema D Michael Goldenberg W Michael Goldenberg C Adam Kimmel

Big (1988), Twentieth Century Fox D Penny Marshall W Gary Ross, Anne Spielberg C Barry Sonnenfeld

Blue in the Face (1995), Miramax Films D Paul Auster, Wayne Wang W Paul Auster, Wayne Wang C Adam Holender

Bonfire of the Vanities, The (1990), Warner Bros. D Brian De Palma W Michael Cristofer, from a novel by Tom Wolfe C Vilmos Zsigmond

Breakfast at Tiffany's (1961), Paramount Pictures D Blake Edwards W George Axelrod, from a novella by Truman Capote C Franz F. Planer, Philip H. Lathrop

Broadway Danny Rose (1984), Orion Pictures D Woody Allen W Woody Allen C Gordon Willis

Brother From Another Planet, The (1984), Cinecom International D John Sayles W John Sayles C Ernest R. Dickerson

Center Stage (2000), Columbia Pictures D Nicholas Hytner W Carol Heikkinen C Geoffrey Simpson

Chasing Amy (1997), Miramax Films D Kevin Smith W Kevin Smith C David Klein

Chelsea Walls (2001), Lions Gate Films D Ethan Hawke W Nicole Burdette, from a play by Nicole Burdette C Tom Richmond

Clockers (1995), Universal Pictures D Spike Lee W Richard Price, Spike Lee, from a novel by Richard Price C Malik Hassan Sayeed

Coogan's Bluff (1968), Universal Pictures D Donald Siegel W Herman Miller, Dean Riesner, Howard Rodman C Bud Thackery

Cotton Comes to Harlem (1970), United Artists D Ossie Davis W Ossie Davis, based on a novel by Chester Himes C Gerald Hirschfield

Cowboy Way, The (1994), Universal Pictures D Gregg Champion W Rob Thompson, Bill Wittliff C Dean Semler

"Crocodile" Dundee (1986), Paramount Pictures D Peter Faiman W John Cornell, Paul Hogan, Ken Shadie C Russell Boyd

"Crocodile" Dundee II (1988), Paramount Pictures D John Cornell W Paul Hogan, Brett Hogan C Russell Boyd

Crooklyn (1994), Paramount Pictures D Spike Lee W Spike Lee, Cinque Lee, Joie Susannah Lee C Arthur Jafa

Crossing Delancey (1987), Warner Bros. D Joan Micklin Silver W Susan Sandler, Steven Kunes C Theo van de Sande

Cruising (1980), United Artists D William Friedkin W William Friedkin, from a novel by Gerald Walker C James A. Contner

Death to Smoochy (2002), Warner Bros. D Danny DeVito W Adam Resnick C Anastas N. Michos

Death Wish (1974), Paramount Pictures D Michael Winner W Wendell Mayes, from a novel by Brian Garfield C Arthur J. Ornitz

Desperately Seeking Susan (1985), MGM D Susan Seidelman W Leora Barish, Floyd Byars C Edward Lachman

Devil's Advocate, The (1997), Warner Bros. D Taylor Hackford W Jonathan Lemkin, Tony Gilroy, from a novel by Andrew Neiderman C Andrzej Bartkowiak

Die Hard: With a Vengeance (1995), Twentieth Century Fox D John McTiernan W Jonathan Hensleigh, Roderick Thorp C Peter Menzies Jr.

Do The Right Thing (1989), Universal Pictures D Spike Lee W Spike Lee C Ernest R. Dickerson

Dog Day Afternoon (1975), Warner Bros. D Sidney Lumet W Frank R. Pierson, from an article by P.F. Kluge, Thomas Moore C Victor J. Kemper

Downtown 81 (originally *New York Beat*) (2001), Twentieth Century Fox D Edo Bertoglio

Eternal Sunshine of the Spotless Mind (2004), Focus Features D Michel Gondry W Charlie Kaufman, Michel Gondry, Pierre Bismuth C Ellen Kuras

Fame (1980), MGM D Alan Parker W Christopher Gore C Michael Seresin

Ferry Tales (2003), HBO Films D Katja Esson W Katja Esson C Katja Esson, Martina Radwan

Fisher King, The (1990), Columbia Pictures D Terry Gilliam W Richard LaGravenese C Roger Pratt

Force of Evil (1948), MGM D Abraham Polonsky W Abraham Polonsky, based on a novel by Ira Wolfert C George Barnes

Fort Apache, the Bronx (1981), Twentieth Century Fox D Daniel Petrie W Heywood Gould C John Alcott

French Connection, The (1971), Twentieth Century Fox D William Friedkin W Ernest Tidyman, Howard Hawks, from a novel by Robin Moore C Owen Roizman

Ghostbusters (1984), Columbia Pictures D Ivan Reitman W Dan Aykroyd, Harold Ramis, Rick Moranis C Laszlo Kovacs

Godfather: Part II, The (1974), Paramount Pictures D Francis Ford Coppola W Francis Ford Coppola, Mario Puzo, from a novel by Mario Puzo C Gordon Willis

Godspell (1973), Columbia Pictures D David Greene W David Greene, John-Michael Tebelak, from a musical play by John-Michael Tebelak C Richard G. Heimann

Godzilla (1998), Columbia Pictures D Roland Emmerich W Ted Elliott, Terry Rossio, Dean Devlin, Roland Emmerich C Ueli Steiger

GoodFellas (1990), Warner Bros. D Martin Scorsese W Nicholas Pileggi, Martin Scorsese, from a book by Nicholas Pileggi C Michael Ballhaus

Green Card (1990), Buena Vista Pictures D Peter Weir W Peter Weir C Geoffrey Simpson

Greetings (1968), Sigma III Corp. D Brian De Palma W Brian De Palma, Charles Hirsch C Robert Fiore

Hair (1979), United Artists D Milos Forman W Gerome Ragni, James Rado, Michael Weller, from a musical play by Gerome Ragni, James Rado, Michael Weller C Miroslav Ondrícek

Hannah and Her Sisters (1986), Orion Pictures D Woody Allen W Woody Allen C Carlo Di Palma

Heights (2004), Sony Pictures Classics D Chris Terrio W Amy Fox, Chris Terrio C Jim Denault

Hitch (2005), Columbia Pictures D Andy Tennant W Kevin Bisch C Andrew Dunn

Hours, The (2002), Paramount Pictures D Stephen Daldry W David Hare, from a novel by Michael Cunning-ham C Seamus McGarvey

Hudson Hawk (1991), Columbia Pictures D Michael Lehmann W Bruce Willis, Robert Kraft, Steven E. de Souza, Daniel Waters C Dante Spinotti

I Like It Like That (1994), Columbia Pictures D Darnell Martin W Darnell Martin C Alexander Gruszynski

I Shot Andy Warhol (1996), Samuel Goldwyn Company D Mary Harron W Mary Harron, Daniel Minahan, Jeremiah Newton, C Ellen Kuras

Inside Man (2006), Universal Pictures D Spike Lee W Russell Gewirtz C Matthew Libatique

Interpreter, The (2005), Universal Pictures D Sydney Pollack W Martin Stellman, Brian Ward, Charles Ran-dolph, Scott Frank, Steven Zaillian C Darius Khondji

It Could Happen to You (1994), Columbia Pictures D Andrew Bergman W Jane Anderson C Carter Burwell

Jeremy (1973), United Artists D Arthur Barron W Arthur Barron C Paul Goldsmith

Jumpin' at the Boneyard (1992), Twentieth Century Fox D Jeff Stanzler W Jeff Stanzler C Lloyd Steven Goldfine

Jungle Fever (1991), Universal Pictures D Spike Lee W Spike Lee C Ernest Dickerson

Kal Ho Naa Ho (2002), Yash Raj Films Pvt. Ltd. D Nikhil Advani W Niranjan Iyengar, Karan Johar C Amil Mehta

Kids (1995), Shining Excalibur Films D Larry Clark W Larry Clark, Harmony Korine, Jim Lewis C Eric Edwards

Killer's Kiss (1955), United Artists D Stanley Kubrick W Stanley Kubrick, Howard Sackler C Stanley Kubrick

King Kong (1976), Paramount Pictures D John Guillermin W Lorenzo Semple Jr., from a screenplay by Merian C. Cooper and Edgar Wallace C Richard H. Kline

Kissing Jessica Stein (2001), Twentieth Century Fox D Charles Herman-Wurmfeld W Heather Juergensen, Jennifer Westfeldt C Lawrence Sher

Klute (1971), Warner Bros. D Alan Pakula W Andy Lewis, Dave Lewis C Gordon Willis

Kramer vs. Kramer (1979), Columbia Pictures D Robert Benton W Robert Benton, from a novel by Avery Corman C Nestor Almendros

Landlord, The (1970), United Artists D Hal Ashby W Bill Gunn, from a novel by Kristin Hunter C Gordon Willis

Little Fugitive (1953), Joseph Burstyn, Inc. D Ray Ashley, Morris Engel, Ruth Orkin W Ray Ashley, Morris Engel, Ruth Orkin C Morris Engel

Little Manhattan (2005), Twentieth Century Fox D Mark Levin W Jennifer Flackett C Tim Orr

Lost Weekend, The (1945), Paramount Pictures D Billy Wilder W Charles Brackett, Billy Wilder, from a novel by Charles R. Jackson C John F. Seitz

Luv (1967), Columbia Pictures D Clive Donner W Elliott Baker, from a play by Murray Schisgal C Ernest Laszlo

Mad Hot Ballroom (2005), Nickelodeon Movies, Paramount Classics D Marilyn Agrelo W Amy Sewell C Claudia Raschke

Malcolm X (1992), Warner Bros. D Spike Lee W Arnold Perl, Spike Lee, from a memoir by Alex Haley, Malcolm X C Ernest Dickerson

Man Push Cart (2005), Flip Side Film D Ramin Bahrani W Ramin Bahrani C Michael Simmonds

Manhattan (1979), United Artists D Woody Allen W Woody Allen, Marshall Brickman C Gordon Willis

Marty (1955), United Artists D Delbert Mann W Paddy Chayefsky, from a teleplay by Paddy Chayefsky C Joseph LaShelle

Mean Streets (1973), Warner Bros. D Martin Scorsese W Martin Scorsese & Mardik Martin C Kent Wakeford

Men in Black (1997), Columbia Pictures D Barry Sonnenfeld W Ed Solomon, from a comic book by Lowell Cunningham C Don Peterman

Midnight Cowboy (1969), United Artists D John Schlesinger W Waldo Salt, from a novel by James Leo Herlihy C Adam Holender

Mirage (1965), Universal Pictures D Edward Dmytryk W Peter Stone, from a novel by Walter Ericson C Joseph MacDonald

Mo' Better Blues (1990), Universal Pictures D Spike Lee W Spike Lee C Ernest Dickerson

My Dinner With André (1981), New Yorker Films D Louis Malle W André Gregory, Wallace Shawn C Jeri Sopanen

Naked City, The (1948), Universal Pictures D Jules Dassin W Alvert Maltz, Malvin Wald C William Daniels

Next Stop, Greenwich Village (1976), Twentieth Century Fox D Paul Mazursky W Paul Mazursky C Arthur J. Ornitz

Night They Raided Minsky's, The (1968), United Artists D William Friedkin W Norman Lear, Sidney Michaels, Arnold Schulman, from a book by Rowland Barber C Andrew Laszlo

Nighthawks (1981), Universal Pictures D Bruce Malmuth, Gary Nelson W David Shaber, Paul Sylbert C James A. Contner

No Way to Treat a Lady (1968), Paramount Pictures D Jack Smight W John Gay, from a novel by William Goldman C Jack Priestly

North by Northwest (1959), MGM D Alfred Hitchcock W Ernest Lehman C Robert Burks

On the Town (1949), MGM D Stanley Donen, Gene Kelly W Betty Comden, Adolph Green, from a musical play by Betty Comden, Adolph Green, Jerome Robbins C Harold Rosson

On the Waterfront (1954), Columbia Pictures D Elia Kazan W Budd Schulberg, from articles by Malcolm Johnson C Boris Kaufman

One Fine Day (1996), Twentieth Century Fox D Michael Hoffman W Terrel Seltzer, Ellen Simon C Oliver Stapleton

Other People's Money (1991), Warner Bros. D Norman Jewison W Alvin Sargent, from a play by Jerry Sterner C Haskell Wexler

Out-of-Towners, The (1970), Paramount Pictures D Arthur Hiller W Neil Simon C Andrew Laszlo

Panic in Needle Park, The (1971), Twentieth Century Fox D Jerry Schatzberg W James Mills, Joan Didion, John Gregory Dunne C Adam Holender

Pawnbroker, The (1964), American International Pictures D Sidney Lumet W Morton S. Fine, David Friedkin, from a novel by Edward Lewis Wallant C Boris Kaufman

Perfect Murder, A (1998), Warner Bros. D Andrew Davis W Patrick Smith Kelly, from a play by Frederick Knott C Dariusz Wolski

Pick-Up Artist, The (1987), Twentieth Century Fox D James Toback W James Toback C Gordon Willis

Pieces of April (2003), MGM D Peter Hedges W Peter Hedges C Tami Reiker

Prime (2005), Universal Pictures D Ben Younger W Ben Younger C William Rexer

Prisoner of Second Avenue, The (1975), Warner Bros. D Melvin Frank W Neil Simon, from a play by Neil Simon C Philip H. Lathrop

Producers, The (1968), AVCO Embassy Pictures D Mel Brooks W Mel Brooks C Joseph Coffey

Producers, The (2005), Universal Pictures D Susan Stroman W Mel Brooks and Thomas Meehan, from a musical play by Mel Brooks and Thomas Meehan C John Bailey, Charles Minsky

Professional, The (1994), Columbia Pictures D Luc Besson W Luc Besson C Thierry Arbogast

Ragtime (1981), Paramount Pictures D Milos Forman W Michael Weller, from a novel by E.L. Doctorow C Miroslav Ondrícek

Report to the Commissioner (1975), United Artists D Milton Katselas W Abby Mann, Ernest Tidyman, from a novel by James Mills C Mario Tosi

Requiem for a Dream (2000), Artisan Entertainment D Darren Aronofsky W Hubert Selby Jr., Darren Aronofsky, from a novel by Hubert Selby, Jr. C Matthew Libatique

Rosemary's Baby (1968), Paramount Pictures D Roman Polanski W Roman Polanski, from a novel by Ira Levin C William Fraker

Royal Tenenbaums, The (2001), Buena Vista Pictures D Wes Anderson W Wes Anderson, Owen Wilson C Robert D. Yeoman

Saturday Night Fever (1977), Paramount Pictures D John Badham W Norman Wexler, from an article by Nik Cohn C Ralf D. Bode

Searching For Bobby Fischer (1993), Paramount Pictures D Steven Zaillian W Steven Zaillian, from a book by Fred Waitzkin C Conrad L. Hall

Serpico (1973), Paramount Pictures D Sidney Lumet W Waldo Salt, Norman Wexler, from a book by Peter Maas C Arthur J. Ornitz

Seven Year Itch, The (1955), Twentieth Century Fox D Billy Wilder W Billy Wilder, George Axelrod, from a play by George Axelrod C Milton Krasner

Shadows (1959), Lion International Films D John Cassavetes W John Cassavetes C Erich Kollmar

Shaft (1971), MGM D Gordon Parks W Ernest Tidyman, John D. F. Black, from a novel by Ernest Tidyman C Urs Furrer

Shaft (2000), Paramount Pictures D John Singleton W Richard Price, John Singleton, Shane Salerno, based on a novel by Ernest Tidyman C Donald E. Thorin

She's the One (1996), Twentieth Century Fox D Edward Burns W Edward Burns C Frank Prinzi

Siege, The (1998), Twentieth Century Fox D Edward Zwick W Lawrence Wright, Menno Meyjes, Edward Zwick, from a novel by Lawrence Wright C Roger Deakins

Single White Female (1992), Columbia Pictures D Barbet Schroeder W Don Roos, from a novel by John Lutz C Luciano Tovoli

Six Degrees of Separation (1993), MGM D Fred Schepisi W John Guare, from a play by John Guare C Ian Baker

Sleepers (1996), Warner Bros. D Barry Levinson W Barry Levinson, from a novel by Lorenzo Carcaterra C Michael Ballhaus

Smithereens (1982), New Line Cinema D Susan Seidelman W Peter Askin, Ron Nyswaner, Susan Seidelman C Chirine El Khadem

Smoke (1995), Miramax Films D Wayne Wang, Paul Auster W Paul Auster C Adam Holender

Sophie's Choice (1982), Universal Pictures D Alan J. Pakula W Alan J. Pakula, from a novel by William Styron C Nestor Almendros

Spider-Man (2002), Columbia Pictures D Sam Raimi W David Koepp, from a comic book by Stan Lee, Steve Ditko C Don Burgess

Splash (1984), Buena Vista Pictures D Ron Howard W Brian Grazer, Bruce Jay Friedman, Lowell Ganz, Babaloo Mandel, C Don Peterman

Squid and the Whale, The (2005), Samuel Goldwyn Company D Noah Baumbach W Noah Baumbach C Robert D. Yeoman

State of Grace (1990), MGM D Phil Joanou W Dennis McIntyre C Jordan Cronenweth

Sugar Hill (1994), Twentieth Century Fox D Leon Ichaso W Barry Michael Cooper C Bojan Bazelli

Summer Of Sam (1999), Buena Vista Pictures D Spike Lee W Victor Colicchio, Michael Imperioli, Spike Lee C Ellen Kuras

Sweet Home Alabama (2002), Buena Vista Pictures D Andy Tennant W Douglas J. Ebock, C. Jay Cox C Andrew Dunn

Sweet Smell of Success (1957), United Artists D Alexander Mackendrick W Clifford Odets, Ernest Lehman, Alexander Mackendrick C James Wong Howe

Taking of Pelham One Two Three, The (1974), MGM D Joseph Sargent W Peter Stone, from a novel by John Godey C Enrique Bravo, Owen Roizman

Taxi Driver (1976), Columbia Pictures D Martin Scorsese W Paul Schrader C Michael Chapman

Three Days of the Condor (1975), Paramount Pictures D Sydney Pollack W Lorenzo Semple, Jr., David Rayfiel, from a novel by James Grady C Owen Roizman

Thousand Clowns, A (1965), United Artists D Fred Coe W Herb Gardner, from a play by Herb Gardner C Arthur J. Ornitz

Times Square (1980), Associated Film Distribution D Allan Moyle W Jacob Brackman, Allan Moyle, Leanne Unger C James A. Contner

Tootsie (1982), Columbia Pictures D Sydney Pollack W Robert Garland, Larry Gelbart, Barry Levinson, Elaine May, Don McGuire, Murray Schisgal C Owen Roizman

Unmarried Woman, An (1978), Twentieth Century Fox D Paul Mazursky W Paul Mazursky C Arthur J. Ornitz

Up the Down Staircase (1967), Warner Bros. D Robert Mulligan W Tad Mosel, from a novel by Bel Kaufman C Joseph F. Coffey

Up the Sandbox (1972), National General Pictures D Irvin Kershner W Paul Zindel, from a novel by Anne Richardson Roiphe C Gordon Willis

INDEX

PHOTO CREDITS

12 Angry Men, P 40 Courtesy of Photofest.

13 Going on 30, P 239 Courtesy of Everett Collection, Inc.

15 Minutes, P 82 © MMI, New Line Productions, Inc. All Rights Reserved. Photo by Phillip V. Caruso. Photo appears courtesy of New Line Productions, Inc.

25th Hour, P 93, 209 Courtesy of Photofest.

A Perfect Murder, P 141 © Warner Bros., a division of Time Warner Entertainment Company, L.P. All Rights Reserved.

A Thousand Clowns, P 51 Courtesy of Photofest.

Across the Sea of Time, P 4–5 Courtesy of Photofest.

After Hours, P 154 © The Geffen Film Company. Licensed by Warner Bros. Entertainment Inc. All Rights Reserved.

Alice, P 224 © 1990 Orion Pictures Corporation. All Rights Reserved.

American Psycho, P 140 Courtesy of Everett Collection, Inc.

An Unmarried Woman, P 152–153 © 1978 Twentieth Century Fox. All Rights Reserved.

Anderson Tapes, The, P 130 Courtesy of Photofest.

Annie Hall, P 114 (black and white) Courtesy of Photofest. P 114 (color), 121, 136, 221 © 1977 Metro-Goldwyn-Mayer Studios Inc. All Rights Reserved.

April Fools, The, P 70 Courtesy of Everett Collection, Inc.

April Fools, The, P 142 Courtesy of Photofest.

As Good As It Gets, P 206 Courtesy of Photofest.

Barefoot in the Park, P 74–75 Courtesy of Photofest.

Basketball Diaries, The, P 199 Courtesy of Photofest.

Basquiat, P 187 Courtesy of Photofest.

*batteries not included, P 190 © 1987 Universal Pictures.

Bed of Roses, P 230–231 © MCMXCVI, New Line Productions, Inc. All Rights Reserved. Photo by Lou Goldman. Photo appears courtesy of New Line Productions, Inc.

Big, P 162–163 Courtesy of Photofest.

Blue in the Face, P 177 Courtesy of Miramax Film Corp. All Rights Reserved.

Bonfire of the Vanities, The P 126, 227 © Warner Bros. Inc. All Rights Reserved. P 226 © 1990 Warner Bros. Inc, All Rights Reserved.

Breakfast at Tiffany's, P 48–49 Courtesy of Everett Collection, Inc.

Broadway Danny Rose, P 158 Courtesy of Photofest.

"Broadway Tribute" Commercial for the 2001 Tony Awards and Visa, P 261 © 2006 Visa U.S.A. Inc.

Brother From Another Planet, The, P 159 Courtesy of Photofest.

"Cagney & Lacey," P 256 Courtesy of Photofest.

Center Stage, P 215 © 2000 Columbia Pictures Industries, Inc. All Rights Reserved. Courtesy of Sony Pictures Entertainment.

Chasing Amy, P 188 Courtesy of Miramax Film Corp. All Rights Reserved.

Chelsea Walls, P 242 Courtesy of Everett Collection, Inc.

Clockers, P 178 Courtesy of Photofest.

Commercial for Nike, P 260 Courtesy of Nike, Inc.

Coogan's Bluff, P 95 Courtesy of Photofest.

Cotton Comes to Harlem, P 100 © 1970 Samuel Goldwyn Productions. All Rights Reserved.

Cowboy Way, The, P 83 © 1994 Universal City Studios, Inc.

"Crocodile" *Dundee,* P 162 Courtesy of Photofest.

"Crocodile" *Dundee II,* P 133 Courtesy of Photofest.

Crooklyn, P 190 Courtesy of Photofest.

Crossing Delancey, P 198 © Warner Bros. Inc. All Rights Reserved.

Cruising, P 78, 144 Courtesy of Photofest.

Death to Smoochy, P 10–11, 238 © Warner Bros., a division of Time Warner Entertainment Company, L.P. All Rights Reserved.

Death Wish, P 67 Courtesy of Photofest.

Desperately Seeking Susan, P 119 (top) Courtesy of Photofest. P 119 (bottom) © 1985 Orion Pictures Corporation. All Rights Reserved. P 156 Courtesy of Everett Collection, Inc.

Devil's Advocate, The, P 226, 233 © Warner Bros. Productions Limited, Monarchy Enterprises B.V. and Regency Entertainment (USA) Inc. All Rights Reserved.

Die Hard: With a Vengeance, P 80–81 Courtesy of Photofest.

Do the Right Thing, P 174 (top only) © 1989 Universal City Studios, Inc. P 174, 175 (bottom two) Courtesy of Photofest.

Dog Day Afternoon, P 6–7, 63, 64–65 © Warner Bros. Inc. All Rights Reserved.

Downtown 81 (originally) *New York Beat,* P 125 Courtesy of Photofest.

Eternal Sunshine of the Spotless Mind, P 250–251 Courtesy of Everett Collection, Inc.

Fame, P 115, 122 © Turner Entertainment Co. A Warner Bros. Entertainment Company. All Rights Reserved.

Ferry Tales, P 196–197 Courtesy of Everett Collection, Inc.

Fisher King, The, P 170–171 Courtesy of Photofest.

Force of Evil, P 33 Courtesy of Getty Images.

Fort Apache, the Bronx, P 126 Courtesy of Everett Collection, Inc.

French Connection, The, P 61, 84–85 © 1971 Twentieth Century Fox. All Rights Reserved.

ACKNOWLEDGMENTS

First and foremost, we would like to thank Mayor Michael R. Bloomberg for fostering a creative, entrepreneurial environment in which to work, and for giving the Mayor's Office of Film, Theatre and Broadcasting the chance to make a difference.

The earliest proposals for this book emerged from conversations with Jon Kamen at @radical.media (whose talented team created the logo design for our "Made in NY" program and for the Mayor's Office itself). Barbaralee Diamonstein-Spielvogel, a dedicated, civic-minded New Yorker, was also crucial in getting this project off the ground. We thank them both enormously for their advice, creative spirit, and support.

At the Mayor's Office, project manager Kara Alaimo helped to keep the book focused and on schedule, and brought her editorial skills, dedication, and attention to detail to its successful completion. Ryan Rumage provided crucial behind-the-scenes support in his typically conscientious fashion. Our research consultant Patrick Ainslie was always willing to go the extra mile to make sure that we ended up with our first choice of images. And Dan Vatsky, our other research associate, worked diligently to help locate and keep track of hundreds of images in connection with the book. At the New York City Law Department, Katherine Winningham proved invaluable for her exceptional counsel, speed-of-light responses and late-night work on this project. Many, many thanks to them all.

Charles Miers, the publisher of Rizzoli International Publications, Inc., shared our vision and excitement for this book from the moment we proposed it, and was unfazed by the tight schedule that its production would entail. Leah Whisler, our editor, worked long hours and many late nights to make sure it all came together in the end. The book literally would not have been possible without them, and we deeply appreciate everything they have done to make it a success.

At Pentagram, Michael Bierut and Armin Vit developed and executed the book's inspired and elegant design with the highest degree of professionalism and dedication. Our debt to them is immense.

The Mayor's Office of Film, Theatre and Broadcasting has undergone a dramatic transformation over the past three years, in no small part thanks to the expertise and dedication of Deputy Commissioner John Battista and Assistant Commissioner Julianne Cho. We would also like to recognize the efforts of Skip Piscitelli, the city's director of state legislative affairs, whose ongoing support and attention to detail led to the swift passage of the tax credit which enhanced the "Made in NY" program.

Our heartfelt thanks go to Ingrid Bernstein for her extraordinary patience and support while this book was being edited, to Lydia Wills at the Paradigm agency for her sage and thoughtful assistance on business and publishing matters, to Eliot R. Brown for carefully combing the completed text for technical errors, and to Jeffrey Keiler at Outpost Digital, who pulled last-minute screen grabs with a smile. Howard and Ron Mandelbaum at Photofest not only provided many of the unusual images in the book, but gave special commercial consideration to the project, which we appreciate greatly.

Many extraordinary individuals in the film industry and city government gave us their valuable time for interviews—which proved so crucial an element of this book—and we wish to salute them here: David Blake, Barry Gottehrer, Brian Hamill, Mary Harron, Adam Holender, Jay Kriegel, Joy Manhoff Flink, Sol Negrin, Molly Ringwald, Abe Schrager, Mary I. Vogt, Jennifer Westfeldt, and Dick Wolf. Thanks to John Amman at the International Guild of Cinematographers and Matt Miller at the Association of Independent Commercial Producers for their efforts to connect us with sources for interviews and images.

We owe special thanks to Martin Scorsese and Nora Ephron for their extraordinary contributions to this book. And great thanks as well to Woody Allen and Sarah Allentuch for allowing us access to images from Mr. Allen's archives.

The images in this book could not have been located, assembled, and licensed without the efforts and hard work of many archivists and stills licensing staff members at motion picture studios, television networks, photo and advertising agencies, and other sources, and we would like to take the opportunity to thank them all individually: At @radical.media, Jon Kamen, Geoff Reinhard, and India Hammer. At IDP Films, Kristi Avram and Greg Johnson. At Paramount, Brian Palagallo. At Disney, Margaret Adamic. At Nike, Keli Richardson. At HBO, Suzanne Quadara, James John Kerigan, and Tobe Becker. At MGM, Barry Dagestino, Jose Simental, Debbie Takami, Maggie Adams, and Sue Peck. At Universal Studios, Roni Lubiner, Cindy Chang, and Diedre Thieman. At Columbia TriStar/Sony, Margarita Diaz, Monique Diaz, and Gilbert Emralino. At CBS, Nancy Eichenbaum. At Twentieth Century-Fox, Andy Bandit and Rob Esterla. At Warner Bros.,Julie Heath, Darlene Grodske, and Jeff Briggs. At New Line Cinema, Robin Zlatin, Hellene Cornell, and Amy Rivera. At Miramax, Julie Daccord, Amy Rocen, and Lori Shamah. At the Weinstein Company, Gil Torres, and Tucker Christon. At the American Museum of the Moving Image, Megan Forbes. At the Sesame Workshop, Maria Maiurro. At Marvel Entertainment, Carol Platt. And at the Everett Collection, Ron Harvey, Joan Moore, and Eva Povzea. We would like to thank David Lee for helping us locate his image from *Mo' Better Blues*, Jonathan Sanger and Neal Preston for their help with images from *The Producers* and *Vanilla Sky*, Anadil Hossain for her help with the images from *Kal Ho Naa Ho*, and Richard I. Leher and Randy Skinner for their assistance in licensing the images from the Rolling Stones' "Love is Strong" video. Our apologies in advance to anyone we have inadvertently omitted from this list.

And finally, our warmest appreciation to the entertainment companies and cultural institutions that very generously donated images from their collections to help make this project possible: the American Museum of the Moving Image, Columbia Tri-Star/Sony Pictures Entertainment, Disney, Dharma Productions, Getty Images, HBO, IDP Films, Metro-Goldwyn-Mayer, Miramax Film Corp., NBC Universal, New Line Cinema, Nike, Paramount, @radical.media, Sesame Street Workshop, Shining Excalibur Films, TBWA/CHIAT/DAY, Twentieth Century Fox, Warner Bros., and the Weinstein Company. We cannot express how grateful we are for your help and support.

KATHERINE OLIVER AND JAMES SANDERS
New York City, June 2006

A NOTE ON THE CONTRIBUTORS

JAMES SANDERS, an architect and filmmaker, is the author of *Celluloid Skyline: New York and the Movies*. With Ric Burns, he co-wrote the Emmy Award-winning PBS series "New York: A Documentary Film" and its companion volume, *New York: An Illustrated History*. He has written for the *New York Times*, the *Los Angeles Times*, *Vanity Fair* and *Architectural Record* and has designed private commissions and public projects in New York, New Jersey, California and elsewhere. In 2006 he was awarded a Guggenheim Fellowship for research in the experience of cities.

MARTIN SCORSESE is one of the most prominent and influential filmmakers of the twentieth century. He directed the critically acclaimed, award-winning films *Taxi Driver*, *Mean Streets*, *Raging Bull*, *The Last Temptation of Christ*, *GoodFellas*, *Gangs of New York* and *The Aviator*. In 1990, he helped establish The Film Foundation, a non-profit organization dedicated to preserving motion picture history.

NORA EPHRON is a journalist, novelist, playwright, screenwriter, and director. Her credits include *Heartburn*, *When Harry Met Sally...*, *Sleepless in Seattle*, *You've Got Mail*, and *Imaginary Friends*. Her latest book, *I Feel Bad About My Neck: And Other Thoughts on Being a Woman*, released in 2006. She lives in New York City.

KATHERINE L. OLIVER was appointed as Commissioner of the New York City Mayor's Office of Film, Theatre and Broadcasting in 2002. The MOFTB markets New York City as a location for entertainment production, develops incentive programs for the industry, and facilitates production throughout the city's five boroughs. Prior to her appointment, Oliver served as General Manager of Bloomberg Radio and Television, where she built digital broadcast operations in twenty-five cities worldwide. She was also a broadcast anchor and producer and taught journalism at New York University.

...ART MY BROTHER MY DEMON LOVER MY DINNER WITH ANDRE MY FATHER, THE HERO MY FAVORITE YEAR MY GIANT MY NAME IS TANINO MY NEW GUN MY SISTE... VE STORY NATALIA NATHAN GRIMM NATIONAL TREASURE NATURAL ENEMIES NÁVRAT ZTRACENÉHO RÁJE NECROPOLIS NEIGHBORS NEMA AVIONA NA ZAGREB N... W ROSE HOTEL NEW YORK CROSSING NEW YORK MINUTE NEW YORK NIGHTS NEW YORK STORIES NEW YORK, NEW YORK NEW YORK'S FINEST NEXT STOP, GREE... GHT SHIFT NIGHT VISIONS NIGHTHAWKS NIGHTMARE NIGHTSTICK NINGÉN NO SHOMEI NO BIG DEAL NO DEPOSIT, NO RETURN NO EXIT NO LOOKING BACK NO MO... ISES OFF NOLA NOON BLUE APPLES NORTH NOT A DAY GOES BY NOT AFRAID TO SAY NOT EVEN THE TREES NOT FOR PUBLICATION NOTHING BUT TROUBLE NOTH... EAR DAY YOU CAN SEE FOREVER ON THE EDGE ON THE Q.T. ON THE ROAD WITH JUDAS ON THE RUN ONCE AGAIN ONCE AROUND ONCE IN THE LIFE ONCE IS NOT E... E LAST DANCE ONE LAST THING ... ONE LOVE ONE MORE KISS ONE NIGHT STAND ONE THIRD ONE TRICK PONY ONE TRUE THING ONLY WHEN I LARF ONLY WHEN I... ONEY OTHER VOICES OUR SONG OUT FOR JUSTICE OUT OF CONTROL OUT OF IT OUTRAGEOUS FORTUNE OUTTAKES OVER THE BROOKLYN BRIDGE OVERNIGHT SE... UTH PARTING GLANCES PARTY GIRL PARTY MONSTER PASSION OF MIND PATERNITY PECKER PELICAN BRIEF PENELOPE PENN & TELLER GET KILLED PENNY ANTE... ONE BOOTH PI PICTURE PERFECT PICTURES OF LILY PIECES OF APRIL PIGEONS PIÑERO PIPE DREAM PITSTOP PIYAR NASEEBAN DA PLAN B PLANES, TRAINS AND... SS POLLOCK POOTIE TANG POP LIFE POPI PORTFOLIO PORTNOY'S COMPLAINT POUND POWER POWER PLAY PREACHING TO THE CHOIR PREMIUM PREPPIES PRES... IVILEGE PRIZZI'S HONOR PROZAC NATION PULSE PULSE: A STOMP ODYSSEY PUNCH THE CLOCK PUNCHLINE PUPPET PURPLE PASTURES PURPLE VIOLETS PURSI... ISIS QUEEN OF THE STARDUST BALLROOM QUEENS LOGIC QUICK CHANGE QUICKSAND QUICKSILVER QUID PRO QUO QUIET COOL QUIZ SHOW R XMAS R.S.V.P. RA... AL: THE MOVIE RECESS RECIPE FOR DISASTER RED DOORS REDS REFLECTIONS IN A GOLDEN EYE REGARDING HENRY RELIGION, INC REMEDY REMEMBERING M... REAM RESCUING DESIRE RESTAURANT RETURN TO PARADISE RETURN TO SALEM'S LOT REUBEN, REUBEN REUNION REVENGE, INC. REVERSAL OF FORTUNE REVO... GGED RIGHT ON! RIOT ON 42ND STREET RIPE ROAD ROADIE ROBERTA ROBOT HOLOCAUST ROBOT STORIES ROCK 'N' ROLL FRANKENSTEIN ROCKAWAY ROCKY RO... BY ROSHNI ROUND MIDNIGHT ROUNDERS ROW YOUR BOAT RUDE AWAKENING RUM AND COKE RUMOR HAS IT... RUNAWAY BRIDE RUNNING RUNNING ON EMPT... VING FACE SAY YOU'LL BE MINE SCAR CITY SCARECROW IN A GARDEN OF CUCUMBERS SCARFACE SCARING THE FISH SCARRED CITY SCENES FROM A MALL SCE... ARCHING FOR PARADISE SEASONS IN THE SUN SECRET LIFE OF AN AMERICAN WIFE SECRET SINS SECRET WINDOW SEE NO EVIL, HEAR NO EVIL SEE YOU IN THE... M SEVEN DEADLY SINS SEVEN MINUTES IN HEAVEN SEVERANCE SEX & THE OTHER MAN SEX APPEAL SEX O'CLOCK NEWS, THE SEXINA: POPSTAR P.I. SEXLAND S... INGS SHE-DEVIL SHEETROCK SHEILA LEVINE IS DEAD AND LIVING IN NEW YORK SHELTER SHELTER ISLAND SHERRYBABY SHE'S THE ONE SHIRLI-MYRLI SHIVER... OPLE SI' LARABY SIAO NU XIAO YU SID AND NANCY SIDE STREETS SIDEWALKS OF NEW YORK SILENCE OF THE LAMBS SILENT PREY SIMON SIMPLY IRRESISTIBL... E WORLD OF TOMORROW SLAM SLAMMER GIRLS SLAVES OF NEW YORK SLAYGROUND SLEEPER SLEEPERS SLEEPING IN A DREAM SLEEPING TOGETHER SLEEPW... APPED SO FINE SOAPDISH SOHO THEY CALL IT SOLILOQUY SOME FISH CAN FLY SOME OF MY BEST FRIENDS ART SOMEBODY KILLED HER HUSBAND SOMEONE... METIME IN AUGUST SOMEWHERE IN THE CITY SOPHIE'S CHOICE SORCERER SORRY, HATERS SOUL MATES SOUND BARRIER SOUP FOR ONE SOUR GRAPES SPAC... ANDOFF STANLEY CUBA STAR '81 STAR! STAR! STARDUST MEMORIES STARS AND BARS STARTING OVER STATE OF GRACE STATES OF CONTROL STATESIDE STAY STA... AD STONEWALL STOREFRONT HITCHCOCK STRANGE INVADERS STRANGERS STRANGERS WITH CANDY STRAYS STREET HUNTER STREET JUSTICE STREET SMART S... IENDS SUCKER PUNCH SUDDEN MANHATTAN SUE SUFFERING BASTARDS SUITS SUMMER OF SAM SUMMER WISHES, WINTER DREAMS SUNDAY SUPER TROOPE... WIMFAN SWITCH SYRIANA SZCZESLIWEGO NOWEGO JORKU TABLE FOR FIVE TABLE ONE TADPOLE TAKE ANOTHER LOOK TAKE THE BRIDGE TAKE THE MONEY AND R... MPORARY GIRL TEN HUNDRED KINGS TEN MINUTES OLDER TERMS OF ENDEARMENT TERROR FIRMER THAT OLD FEELING THAT'S ADEQUATE THAT'S DANCING! TH... RERS THE ADVENTURES OF ROCKY & BULLWINKLE THE ADVENTURES OF SEBASTIAN COLE THE AMAZING FLOYDINI THE AMERICAN ASTRONAUT THE AMERICAN R... SKETBALL DIARIES THE BAXTER THE BEAT THE BEAUTIFUL COUNTRY THE BEAUTY ACADEMY OF KABUL THE BELIEVER THE BELIEVERS THE BELL JAR THE BEST M... NE COLLECTOR THE BONFIRE OF THE VANITIES THE BOOK OF LIFE THE BOOKIE'S LAMENT THE BOOST THE BORGIA STICK THE BOSTONIANS THE BOURNE SUPREI... GHT OUT THE BUMBLEBEE FLIES ANYWAY THE BUSINESS OF STRANGERS THE BUTCHER'S WIFE THE C WORD THE CABINET OF DR. RAMIREZ THE CAVEMAN'S VALI... ON THE COOKOUT THE CORRUPTOR THE COTTON CLUB THE COTTONWOOD THE COURT THE CROOKED CORNER THE CROSS AND THE SWITCHBLADE THE CRY THE C... CK THE DEAD GUY'S SON THE DEAL THE DEBTORS THE DEER & THE CHEETAH THE DELI THE DEPARTED THE DETECTIVE THE DEVIL AND DANIEL WEBSTER THE DEV... OISTS THE ELECTRIC URN THE ELEPHANT KING THE EMPATH THE EMPEROR'S CLUB THE END OF THE BEGINNING THE ESCAPE ARTIST THE EXCHANGE THE EXORC... APTER THE FINAL EQUATION THE FIRST DEADLY SIN THE FIRST WIVES CLUB THE FISHER KING THE FORGOTTEN THE FOUR SEASONS THE FRENCH CONNECTION T... OM MONDAY THE GLASS MENAGERIE THE GODFATHER THE GOLDEN BOAT THE GOOD SHEPHERD THE GOODBYE GIRL THE GOODBYE PEOPLE THE GREAT GATSBY... CHIE THE HARD PLACE THE HARD WAY THE HAWK IS DYING THE HEADHUNTER'S SISTER THE HEADLESS EYES THE HEARTBREAK KID THE HEBREW HAMMER THE... E HUNGER THE HURRICANE THE ICE STORM THE IDOLMAKER THE IMAGEMAKER THE IMPOSTORS THE INCIDENT THE INDEPENDENT THE IN-LAWS THE INTERPRE... USTARD MAN THE KILLING OF JOHN LENNON THE KILLING ZONE THE KILL-OFF THE KING OF COMEDY THE KINGS OF BROOKLYN THE KNEE SHACK THE KREMLIN LE... E LAST SUPPER THE LAUGHING MAN THE LAVERNE AFFAIR THE LEGACY OF WALTER FRUMM THE LEMON SISTERS THE LINGUINI INCIDENT THE LONELY GUY THE L... NGS THE MAN IN THE GLASS BOOTH THE MAN IN THE MOON THE MAN WHO CAME TO DINNER THE MAN WHO FELL TO EARTH THE MAN WHO LOVED WOMEN THE MA... CES THE MISADVENTURES OF MARGARET THE MISSION THE MONEY PIT THE MONEY SHOT THE MONEY TRAIN THE MOTEL THE MUPPETS TAKE MANHATTAN THE M... STENER THE NIGHT THEY RAIDED MINSKY'S THE NINTH GATE THE NOTORIOUS BETTIE PAGE THE OBJECT OF MY AFFECTION THE OCCULTIST THE ODD COUPLE THE... E PAPER THE PEACE! DVD THE PEACEMAKER THE PEOPLE NEXT DOOR THE PERFECT MAN THE PHOTOGRAPHER THE PICKLE THE PICK-UP ARTIST THE PICTURE OF... EENWICH VILLAGE THE PORNOGRAPHER: A LOVE STORY THE POSSESSION OF JOEL DELANEY THE PREACHER'S WIFE THE PRINCE OF TIDES THE PRISONER OF SI... ONDE THE REALITY TRAP THE REAWAKENING THE REEL THE REFRIGERATOR THE REFUGE THE RETURN OF CAPTAIN INVINCIBLE THE REUNION THE RIDE THE RITZ... NTISTS THE SECRET OF MY SUCCESS THE SENTINEL THE SEVEN-UPS THE SHAMAN THE SHOW THE SICILIAN CLAN THE SIEGE THE SIMIAN LINE THE SISTER THE S... A BAD BOY THE STUFF THE SUBJECT WAS ROSES THE SUBSTANCE OF FIRE THE SUBSTITUTE 2: SCHOOL'S OUT THE SUCKLING THE SUICIDE CLUB THE SUITORS TH... O THREE THE TALENTED MR. RIPLEY THE TAVERN THE TAXMAN THE TECHNICAL WRITER THE TELEPHONE BOOK THE TENANTS THE THING ABOUT MY FOLKS THE TH... E TWO HENRYS THE ULTIMATE SOLUTION OF GRACE QUIGLEY THE UNBELIEVABLE TRUTH THE UNDERCOVER MAN THE UNDERDOG THE UNDERTAKER THE USUAL S... UGS THE WAR WITHIN THE WARRIOR CLASS THE WARRIORS THE WATERSHED THE WAY WE LIVE NOW THE WAY WE WERE THE WEATHER MAN THE WHITE WHORE R... ON THEORY OF ACHIEVEMENT THERE'S GOOD WEATHER IN DERIBASOVSKAYA THEY ALL LAUGHED THEY CALL ME BRUCE? THEY MIGHT BE GIANTS THEY'RE JUST... REE DAYS OF THE CONDOR THREE THE HARD WAY THREE WOMEN THRILLED TO DEATH THROWING DOWN TIE A YELLOW RIBBON TILL PROVEN INNOCENT TILL THE... YESTERDAY TOMORROW TOKKAN TOMMY HOBSON & THE LOVE SUPREME TOMORROW NIGHT TONG HAU GOO SI TONIGHT AT NOON TONY 'N' TINA'S WEDDING TO... UNTRY TOWN DIARY TRACKS TRADING PLACES TRANSAMERICA TRANSFORMATIONS TREASURE TREES LOUNGE TRIBUTE TRICK TRIFLING WITH FATE TRIPLE BOGE... LIEVER TRUE COLORS TRUE CONVICTIONS TRUE IDENTITY TRUE LOVE TRUE VINYL TRUST ME TRUST THE MAN TUMBE TUMSA NAHIN DEKHA TURBULENCE TURK 1... OPLE TWO WEEKS NOTICE U.S. MARSHALS UN AMOUR DE SORCIÈRE UN ARGENTINO EN NEW YORK UN DIVAN À NEW YORK UN ITALIANO IN AMERICA UNBRIDLED... UX/ONE WOMAN OR UNFAITHFUL UNFAITHFULLY YOURS UNFORESEEN UNHOLY UNION SQUARE UP THE DOWN STAIRCASE UP THE SANDBOX URBAN SAFARI URE... MOOTH VENGEANCE VENUS IN FURS VETTAIYADU VILLAIYADU VIBES VIGILANTE VINCE AND THE BARNACLES VIOLETTA LA REINE DE LA MOTO VIRGIL BLISS VODKA... ALKER WALKING AND TALKING WALKING ON THE SKY WALL STREET WALLS & BRIDGES WALTER AND HENRY WANNABES WAR OF THE WORLDS WARRIOR QUEEN W... E'LL TAKE MANHATTAN WENT TO CONEY ISLAND ON A MISSION FROM GOD...BE BACK BY FIVE WE'RE TALKING SERIOUS MONEY WEST BANK BROOKLYN WEST NEW... HAT'S SO FUNNY? WHAT'S UP, TIGER LILY? WHAT'S YOUR SIGN? WHEN WHEN HARRY MET SALLY... WHEN NATURE CALLS WHEN TYSON MET TYRA WHEN WILL I BE... THE WHITE WOLF WHITE LIES WHITE MAN'S BURDEN WHITE PALACE WHITE RAT WHITE WATER SUMMER WHITEBOYZ WHO IS HARRY KELLERMAN, AND WHY IS H... LD KINGDOM WILDEST DREAMS WILDLY AVAILABLE WILLARD WILLIE & PHIL WILLIE DYNAMITE WIMPS WINDCROFT WINDOWS WINNING GIRLS THROUGH PSYCHI... FER WOUNDED HEART WRESTLING WITH ALLIGATORS WRITER'S BLOCK WRONG IS RIGHT X X. X-MEN X-PATRIOTS XTACY XX/XY XXL YEAR OF THE DRAGON